THE HUNTING & FISHING LIBRARY®

FISHING NATURAL LAKES

By Dick Sternberg

DICK STERNBERG is well qualified to write about natural lakes. He formerly directed Minnesota's lake survey program, and has spent a lifetime fishing natural lakes of every conceivable type.

CY DECOSSE INCORPORATED
Chairman: Cy DeCosse
President: James B. Maus
Executive Vice President: William B. Jones

FISHING NATURAL LAKES
Author & Project Director: Dick Sternberg
Editor: Greg Breining
Project Manager: Joseph Cella
Senior Art Director: Bradley Springer
Art Director: Dave Schelitzche
Principal Photographer: William Lindner
Staff Photographers: Mike Hehner, Mark Macemon, Mette Nielsen, Cathleen Shannon
Photo Director: Mike Hehner
Photo Assistants: Steve Hauge, Andy Lessin, Jim Moynagh
Research Director: Eric Lindberg
Researchers: Steve Hauge, Mike Hehner, Jim Moynagh
Director of Development, Planning & Production: Jim Bindas
Production Manager: Amelia Merz
Senior Production Artist: Mark Jacobson
Typesetting: Kevin D. Frakes, Linda Schloegel
Production Staff: Janice Cauley, Joe Fahey, Duane John, Yelena Konrardy, Nik Wogstad
Illustrators: Thomas Boll, Bradley Springer
Contributing Photographers: Frank Balthis Photography; Mark Emery; Fred Hirschmann; Les Johnson; Jerry Leach/University of Nebraska; Dr. Robert Megard/University of Minnesota; Minnesota Pollution Control Agency; National Air Photo Library/Energy, Mines & Resources Canada; Radarsat International, Inc.; Dr. Ted Roeder/University of Wisconsin; R. Hamilton Smith Photography; South Florida Water Management District; Dick Sternberg; United States Army Corps of Engineers; United States Fish & Wildlife Service; Wisconsin Dept. of Natural Resources

Cooperating Individuals and Agencies: Skip Adams; Air Saskatchewan Aviation — Gordon Wallace; Bill Alley; Jerry Anderson; Ted Anderson; Arkansas Game & Fish Commission — Keith Sutton; Greg Arnold; Curtis Batts; Glen Bever; Richard Bishop; Charles Bowe; Camp Fish — Dan Cravens, Don Solstad; Canadian Consulate General — Bruce Verner; Paul Dechaine; Greg Eide; Noble Enge; Far North Recreation — Neil, Scott & Todd Moldenhauer; Fishing Hotspots — Steve Brich, Bob Knops; Florida Dept. of Natural Resources — Terry Sullivan; Florida Game & Fresh Water Fish Commission — Smokie Holcomb, Danon Moxley, Tom Schampeau; Rusty Flowers; Butch Furtman; Dave Genz; Mick Greene; Doug Hannon; Don Hatcher; Morgan Henderson; Don Holloway; Dean Jameson; Les Johnson; Sonny Johnson; Bob Jorgenson; Gene Kaiser; Kasba Lake Lodge — Rob Hill; Len Larson; Dave Lindmark; Louisiana Dept. of Wildlife & Fisheries — Mike Wood; Maine Dept. of Inland Fisheries & Wildlife — Peter Bourque, Owen Fenderson, Paul Johnson, Tim Obrey; Metropolitan Council — Dick Osgood; Ed Metzger; Minnesota Dept. of Natural Resources — Harlan Fierstine, Bruce Gilbertson; Mississippi Dept. of Economic Development — Jay Hambright, John Horhn; Mississippi Dept. of Wildlife Conservation — John Burriss, Gary Lucas; New Hampshire Fish & Game Dept. — Carol Henderson; Maurice Niebert; Pat Olson; Ontario Ministry of Natural Resources — H.J. Gibbard, Dennis Wilson; Jerry & Amanda Packard; Bill Petit; Spence Petros; Don Pursch; Gary Robinson; Clif & Betty Santa; Saskatchewan Dept. of Economic Development & Tourism — Gerard Makach; John Seagerson; Eddie Slater; South Dakota Dept. of Game, Fish & Parks — Al Knapp; South Florida Water Management District — Kim O'Dell; Douglas Taft; Reggie Thiel; Paul Thorne; Vic Turner; United States Army Corps of Engineers — John Brooks, Steve Cobb, Charles Elliott, Mike Robinson, Doug Shields; United States Geological Survey — Tom Winter; University of Florida — Karen Brown, Dr. Tom Crisman; University of Minnesota — Dr. Robert Megard; University of Wisconsin — Dr. Jeffery Thornton, Robert Korth; C.E. Williams; Wisconsin Dept. of Natural Resources — Tom Beard, Rick Cornelius

Cooperating Manufacturers: A.C. Shiner, Inc.; Abu-Garcia, Inc.; Bait Barn Worm Farms; Berkley, Inc./Trilene Fishing Line; Bill Lewis Lures; Blue Fox Tackle Corporation; Brell Mar Products, Inc.; Cannon/S & K Products, Inc.; D & K Distributors, Inc.; Daiwa Corporation; Ditto Mfg., Inc.; Eppinger Mfg. Company; Feldmann Eng. & Mfg. Co., Inc.; Fenwick; Fish River Brand Tackle, Inc.; The Gaines Company; GNB, Incorporated/Stowaway Batteries; Herrick Enterprises/Wave Wackers; Hondex Marine Electronics; Johnson Fishing, Inc.; Lindy-Little Joe, Inc.; Lowrance Electronics, Inc.; Lucky Strike Mfg., Inc.; Lund Boats; Mercury Marine-Mariner Outboards; Nordic Crestliner Boat Co.; Normark Corporation; Northland Fishing Tackle; Plano Molding Co.; Poe's; Pointmatic Corporation; Pradco; Producto Lure Co.; St. Croix Rod Co.; Si-Tex Marine Electronics, Inc.; Slater's Jigs; Stratos Boats, Inc.; Stren Fishing Line; Tru-Turn, Inc.; Uncle Josh Bait Company; Winter Fishing Systems; Yamaha Motor Corp., USA

Color Separations: Multi-Scan International Reproduction A/S, Denmark
Printing: R. R. Donnelley & Sons, Co. (0191)

Cy DeCosse Incorporated offers Hunting & Fishing Products at special subscriber discounts. For information write:

Hunting & Fishing Products
5900 Green Oak Drive
Minnetonka, MN 55343

Library of Congress
Cataloging-in-Publication Data

Sternberg, Dick. Fishing natural lakes / by Dick Sternberg.
p. cm. — (The Hunting & fishing library)
Includes index.
ISBN 0-86573-035-0 (hard)
1. Fishing — United States. 2. Fishing — Canada. 3. Fishes, Freshwater — United States. 4. Fishes, Freshwater — Canada. 5. Lakes — United States. 6. Lakes — Canada.
I. Title. II. Series.
SH463.S74 1991   90-19640
799.1'1'0971 — dc20

Contents

Introduction

An astonishing variety of natural lakes dot the earth's surface. They range in size from immense Lake Superior, which covers an area larger than the state of South Carolina, to small ponds where a good cast would land on the opposite shore.

Many authorities have tried to categorize natural lakes into distinct types. They've devised numerous classification schemes, few of which bear much resemblance to the others. Depending on which expert you believe, North America has somewhere from 20 to 100 lake types, representing about 2 million natural lakes. This book will concentrate on the types of natural lakes most important to fishermen.

To narrow the book's focus, we will include only warmwater lakes and "two-story" lakes (those with both warmwater and coldwater fish). We tentatively plan to cover natural lakes with coldwater fish and man-made lakes in future volumes of *The Hunting & Fishing Library.*

The first section of this book, "Understanding Natural Lakes," provides the basic information you need to comprehend the daily, seasonal and long-term changes that all natural lakes undergo, and how these changes affect fish behavior.

We'll explain the complex set of physical and chemical factors that make each lake different, and why these factors cause the same kind of fish to behave differently in different lakes.

The second section, "How to Fish Natural Lakes," concentrates on techniques you can use to catch gamefish in the most important types of lakes. Rather than hypothetical examples of different lake types, we use specific case studies to represent the fishing situations anglers are most likely to encounter.

In each case study, we track the seasonal movements of every important kind of gamefish and show you the best baits, lures, techniques and equipment for catching them in that specific lake type.

You may never fish any of our case-study lakes, but the case studies will probably represent any lake you do fish and will help you master lakes of that type.

The average angler often has trouble adapting to new waters. Fishermen who are considered "legends" on their favorite lake often fail miserably when they try a different type of lake.

Our case-study approach will show you why the fishing techniques that work so well in one type of lake may not work at all in another. Physical and chemical differences between the lakes often cause the fish to occupy different depths, and differences in the forage base usually mean different feeding behavior.

After reading this book, you'll know how to tailor your techniques to suit the type of water you're fishing. Even if you do all of your fishing on one kind of lake, the wide variety of techniques shown will certainly give you some new ideas.

Understanding Natural Lakes

How Natural Lakes Are Formed

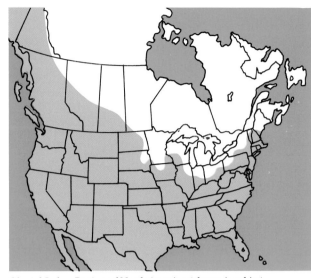

The North American continent has dozens of types of natural lakes formed by different geological processes. The lake types pictured on the pages that follow are of greatest interest to anglers. Reservoirs and other kinds of man-made lakes will not be addressed in this book.

The vast majority of natural lakes in North America were formed by glacial activity. Glaciers formed lakes in many different ways, the most important of which are shown below.

Glacial Lakes Region of North America (shown in white)

How Glacial Lakes Were Formed

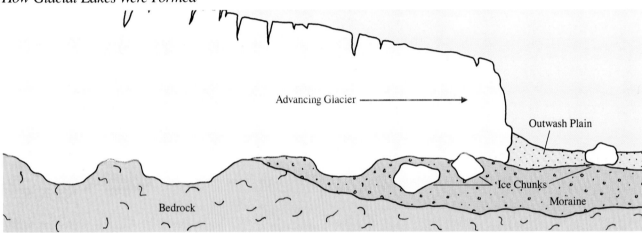

ADVANCING GLACIERS scoured out basins in the bedrock. Some glaciers were more than a mile high, so their excavating force was tremendous. As they moved, they pushed along earthen debris and broken-off ice chunks, forming a *moraine* with an irregular surface ahead of and underneath the mass of ice. As the glacier thawed, rivers of meltwater carried sand, gravel and more ice chunks, depositing them on the *outwash plain*.

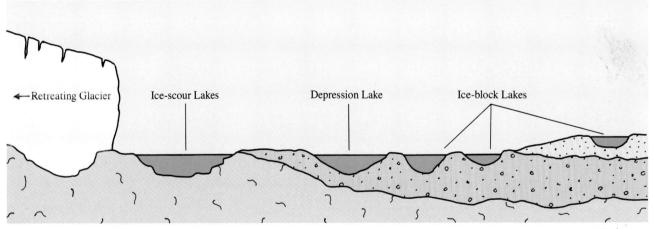

RETREATING GLACIERS left huge chunks of ice buried in the moraine and the outwash plain. Eventually the ice chunks melted, forming *ice-block* lakes. *Ice-scour* lakes formed in the basins cut into the bedrock. The depressions on the irregular surface of the moraine also filled with water to form lakes.

ICE-SCOUR LAKES have bedrock basins because the advancing glacier chiseled away any overlying earthen material. Most of these lakes have filled in very little since they were formed and the bedrock remains exposed.

ICE-BLOCK LAKES, or *kettles*, formed in the outwash plain (left) tend to have rounded, gently sloping basins composed primarily of sand and gravel. Ice-block lakes on the moraine (right) also tend to have rounded basins, but the bottom materials are usually coarser, with more rubble and boulders. Lakes formed in depressions on the moraine (not shown) are difficult to distinguish from ice-block lakes on the moraine.

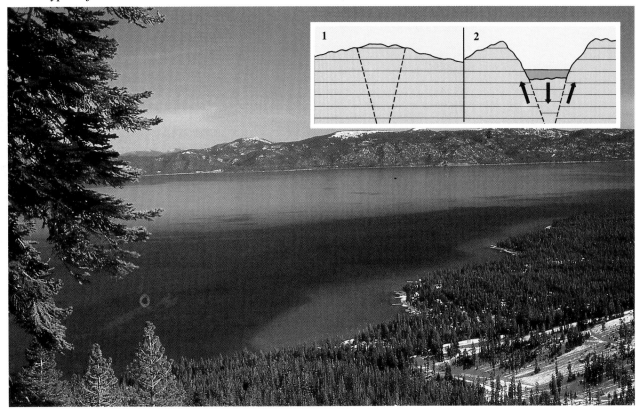

TECTONIC LAKES are formed by movements of the earth's crust. Most commonly, a portion of the earth's surface sinks or tilts, usually along fault lines (inset 1), creating a depression that fills with water (inset 2). Some of the world's largest lakes, such as Lake Baikal in eastern Siberia, were formed this way.

OXBOW LAKES form when winding rivers change course. The insets show how the process works. The river (1) develops a loop, almost doubling back on itself. Then, (2) floodwaters cut a new channel across the sharp bend. Soon, (3) silt fills in the upper end of the old channel, cutting it off from the river. Eventually, (4) the lower end fills in too, leaving a lake that is completely separated from the new river channel.

SOLUTION LAKES form when groundwater dissolves a cavity in the limestone bedrock (inset 1). Eventually, the overlying material collapses, creating a sinkhole (photo above and inset 2). Over time, several sinkholes may combine to form a much larger solution lake. These lakes are the predominant type in Florida.

CRATER LAKES form after a volcano erupts. The materials ejected create a void that fills with water. Lava flows may also dam up valleys, forming lakes. And the hardened lava contains depressions where water collects.

EOLIAN LAKES form when strong winds over extended periods create shallow depressions in loose, sandy soil. The depressions eventually fill with water. Lakes of this type are common in the Nebraska Sandhills.

Dynamics
of Natural Lakes

Each natural lake is unique. Even lakes that seem almost identical often support different kinds of fish, and the locations where you catch fish are different too. Some lakes routinely produce trophy fish, while others are known for "eaters."

You may have wondered why one lake resembles pea soup, while a nearby lake is ultraclear, or why ice-out is always a week earlier on one lake than on another right across the road.

These differences result from a complex web of interrelated chemical and physical properties of the lake, including such things as water temperature, water fertility and oxygen level.

Each of these properties, by itself, tells you little about the lake or its fish population. It's the combined effect that counts.

Just because a lake has plenty of cold water in the depths, for instance, does not necessarily mean it will support coldwater fish. Conditions may be right for coldwater fish 11 months out of the year, but if the oxygen level in the depths sags too low for a few weeks in the summer, coldwater fish cannot survive.

On the following pages, we'll discuss each important chemical and physical property individually, and then we'll show you how the combined effect of these properties influences gamefish behavior.

Of course, chemical and physical conditions in any lake are constantly changing and, as a result, fish behave differently at different times of year. The diagrams on pages 20 to 25 will help you understand why gamefish move about as they do from season to season in three different types of lakes.

Water Temperature

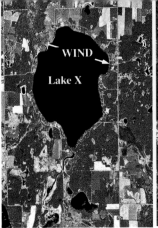

Lake X warms and cools faster than Lake Y because the water is more easily circulated by the wind

Water temperature affects not only what kind of fish live in a lake, but also how fast they grow and how they behave.

A largemouth bass, for instance, grows fastest at about 75° F; a lake trout at about 50. Higher or lower temperatures mean slower growth. How much a fish grows in a given year depends on how long the water remains near the optimum temperature.

Knowledgeable anglers consider water temperature in deciding which lakes to fish, especially in early season. They know that fishing is best in the lakes that warm earliest because the fish are more active. They also know that even minor day-to-day temperature changes affect gamefish feeding patterns.

Following are the factors that have the greatest effect on water temperature:

Surface-to-Volume Ratio. Lakes get most of their heat from the sun and wind warming the surface. They also lose their heat from the surface. The more surface area a lake has in comparison to its volume, the faster the water warms in spring and the faster it cools in fall.

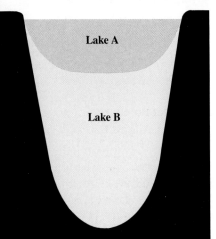

Lake A warms and cools much faster than Lake B because it has more surface area compared to its volume

If two nearby lakes are of similar size and shape, the shallower one has the higher surface-to-volume ratio, so it warms earlier in spring and cools earlier in fall. The shallower lake is a much better choice for early-season fishing; the deep one for late-season fishing.

Exposure to the Wind. Most shallow, bowl-shaped lakes are completely exposed to the wind. They circulate from top to bottom, so they warm and cool more rapidly than deep, narrow lakes, especially those whose long axis is crosswise to the prevailing winds.

Latitude. The maximum summertime surface temperature of a northern lake may be almost as high as that of a similar lake in the South, but the southern lake warms earlier in spring and stays warm later in fall. Because the growing season is longer, fish in the southern lake grow faster.

In the Arctic, lakes are ice free for only two or three months out of the year. Because the surface temperature seldom exceeds 50° F, these waters are best suited to coldwater fish such as lake trout, which grow very slowly and may not mature until the age of 15. Egg development is so slow that they may spawn only once every two or three years.

In the deep South, surface temperatures seldom fall below 60° F, even in midwinter. Fish remain active throughout the year. Only warmwater species such as largemouth bass occur naturally in these waters.

Altitude. Altitude affects water temperature much the same way as latitude. Lakes at high elevations warm later and cool earlier than similar lakes at low elevations.

Source of Water. Except in very small lakes, the water source has little effect on water temperature. Many anglers believe that spring-fed lakes are much colder than other lakes, but this is seldom the case.

Even if a lake is spring fed, heat is absorbed through the surface much faster than springs cool the water. There may be coolwater pockets around the springs, but these have little effect on overall water temperature.

The same is true of coldwater streams entering a lake. There may be a coolwater plume around the mouth of the stream, but unless the stream is very large and the lake very small, the stream cannot contribute enough water to cool the entire lake.

LAKE STRATIFICATION. Most of a lake's heat comes from the sun, so one would expect the temperature to be warmest at the surface and decrease rapidly with depth. But this is rarely the case.

On a calm, sunny day, the surface will be a few degrees warmer than the water just below. But when

Understanding Turnover (illustrations depict fall turnover)   Temperature key: ◼ warm ◼ cool ◻ cold

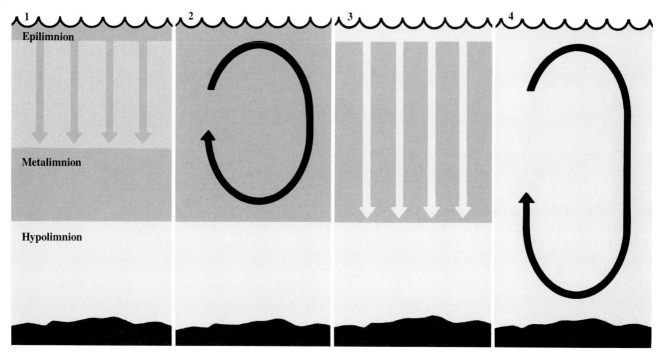

TURNOVER begins when (1) the surface temperature drops and the cooler, denser water starts to sink. Soon, the temperature of the epilimnion is the same as that of the metalimnion, so (2) the wind mixes these layers. As the surface temperature continues to drop, (3) the cold

water begins to sink into the hypolimnion. When the temperature of the upper layer reaches that of the hypolimnion, (4) the wind mixes the water from top to bottom and the turnover is completed. If the oxygen level in the depths was low, it will be replenished during turnover.

the wind starts blowing, the movement of the water distributes the heat uniformly throughout the upper layer of the lake. The thickness of this upper layer, or *epilimnion*, depends mainly on the size of the lake. A large lake generally mixes to a greater depth than a small one; because of the broader sweep, the wind has more mixing power.

Below the epilimnion, the water is cooler and, therefore, denser. So it resists mixing by the wind. The temperature in this middle layer, or *metalimnion*, drops rapidly with depth, and the zone where it drops fastest is called the *thermocline*. Often, the two terms are used interchangeably.

The *hypolimnion* extends from the lower limit of the thermocline to the bottom. Because it is well insulated from the effects of the sun and wind, its temperature is quite uniform.

This three-layer configuration is typical of most natural lakes in North America during the warm months of the year. Such lakes are said to be *stratified*. Only very shallow lakes do not stratify; the wind circulates the water from top to bottom.

Temperature stratification persists well into fall, until the temperature of the epilimnion approaches that of the hypolimnion. As the surface water cools, it becomes denser and sinks. When the upper and

lower layers are at the same temperature and density, even a light wind circulates the entire lake, mixing the water from top to bottom. This phenomenon is called the *fall turnover* (see diagram above).

Exactly when fall turnover takes place varies from lake to lake and year to year. A shallow lake turns over sooner than a deep one; the bottom temperature is warmer, so the surface cools to the same temperature earlier in fall. In a warm fall, it takes longer for the surface to cool, so turnover is later than normal.

Luckily for the aquatic life in northern lakes, water has a unique property that keeps lakes from freezing to the bottom. Like most other substances, water gets heavier as its temperature decreases. But when it drops below 39.2° F, it gets lighter. The colder, lighter water stays on the surface and eventually freezes; the warmer, heavier water stays on bottom.

The bottom water stays warmer than the surface through the winter. But once the lake is ice free, the sun begins warming the surface and the wind circulates the epilimnion until it reaches the same temperature as the hypolimnion. Then, the entire lake begins to mix, resulting in the *spring turnover*.

As the surface continues to warm, the lake again stratifies into three temperature layers that will persist into fall.

FERTILITY of the water can be judged by the amount of phytoplankton (left inset) and zooplankton (right inset) it contains. In a highly fertile lake, a heavy algae bloom in summer leaves a dense layer of green scum on the surface.

Water Fertility

Water fertility has some important consequences for gamefish. It governs how much food the lake produces and thus how fast the fish grow. It affects the clarity and oxygen content of the water, so it influences where the fish are found. It also determines how fast the lake *ages*, or fills in with sediments.

Fertility depends on the amount of nutrients, such as phosphorus and nitrogen, in the water. Just as these nutrients cause grass to grow in your lawn, they make algae, or *phytoplankton*, grow in a lake. The algae, in turn, serves as food for microscopic animals, or *zooplankton*. These organisms, collectively called *plankton*, are the primary links in the aquatic food chain.

Plankton has a dramatic effect on water clarity. Researchers measure clarity with a Secchi disk, an 8-inch disk divided into alternating black and white quarters. The disk is lowered into the water and the depth at which it is no longer visible is the Secchi disk reading.

In spring, a lake may have a Secchi disk reading of 10 feet or more, but by midsummer, *algae blooms* reduce the reading to only a few inches. As the water cools in fall, the algae blooms subside and clarity increases.

OLIGOTROPHIC LAKES don't produce much plankton. Because there is little sediment on the bottom, their basins are deep. They have sparse growths of aquatic vegetation and produce only small crops of fish.

MESOTROPHIC LAKES have more plankton and thus more sediment than oligotrophic lakes; less than eutrophic lakes. They're intermediate in depth, amount of weed growth and production of fish.

EUTROPHIC LAKES have huge plankton crops, which result in thick sediment deposits on the bottom. They're shallow and weedy, and produce more pounds of fish per acre than other types of lakes.

A good index of the fertility of a lake is the phosphorus content, which is measured in terms of *total phosphorus*.

Poorly nourished, or *oligotrophic*, lakes have low nutrient levels. Total phosphorus is usually below 15 ppb (parts per billion). Well-nourished, or *eutrophic*, lakes contain high levels of dissolved nutrients. Total phosphorus generally measures more than 50 ppb. *Mesotrophic* lakes have intermediate nutrient levels. Total phosphorus ranges from 15 to 50 ppb.

Because of their low fertility, oligotrophic lakes age more slowly than other lakes. Less organic matter is produced, so less dies and accumulates on the bottom. Consequently, oligotrophic lakes have the deepest, coldest water.

As the sediment level builds up on the bottom of an oligotrophic lake, it gradually gets shallower and warmer until it becomes a mesotrophic lake; a mesotrophic lake gets shallower and warmer yet, until it becomes eutrophic.

As the aging process continues, the sediment layer becomes so thick that the lake is too shallow to support fish.

Many believe that all lakes are oligotrophic when first formed, then become eutrophic over time. But such is not the case. An ice-block lake on a moraine, for instance, generally has a high nutrient level shortly after formation, the result of minerals dissolved from the surrounding watershed and from the lake basin itself.

Dissolved Oxygen

For fish to survive and behave normally, the water must contain adequate dissolved oxygen. Most fish species require a dissolved oxygen concentration of about 5 ppm for long-term survival. Some roughfish can survive on a little less; some salmonids need a little more.

Most dissolved oxygen gets into the water in two ways: from agitation by the wind, and from photosynthesis by aquatic plants. Some may enter from tributary streams.

In early spring, a lake is thoroughly mixed, so the water is saturated with oxygen from top to bottom. But as the season progresses, dissolved oxygen is used up by the organisms inhabiting the lake. Among these are the bacteria decomposing organic matter on the lake bottom.

Oxygen is quickly replenished in the shallows through mixing by the wind and photosynthesis of aquatic plants. But the wind does not circulate oxygen into the depths, and few plants grow there, so oxygen is not replenished.

How fast the oxygen is consumed depends mainly on the fertility of the water. In a eutrophic lake, for instance, the total production of aquatic life may exceed that of an oligotrophic lake by 20 times. And because more organisms are produced, more are dying and sinking to the bottom where bacteria consume tremendous amounts of oxygen during the decomposition process.

Not only do eutrophic lakes contain more organic matter to consume oxygen, their depths are much warmer, so the consumption rate is considerably greater. In a eutrophic lake with a bottom temperature of 75° F, for example, a given organism would consume about four times as much oxygen as in an oligotrophic lake with a bottom temperature of 45. As a result, oxygen may be consumed 80 times faster than in an oligotrophic lake.

Furthermore, warm water cannot hold as much dissolved oxygen as cold water. At a temperature of 45° F, the water can hold 12 ppm; at 75° F, only 8.5 ppm.

In most stratified eutrophic lakes, oxygen levels in the depths start to wane by early summer, so gamefish are forced into shallow water. As a result, these lakes are best suited for warmwater fish. Even if the depths were cold enough, which they usually aren't, coldwater fish could not survive because of the oxygen shortage.

Oligotrophic lakes, on the other hand, have plenty of dissolved oxygen from top to bottom throughout the year. They are best suited for coldwater fish, although warmwater fish sometimes inhabit the shallower zones.

Mesotrophic lakes have dissolved oxygen to greater depths than eutrophic lakes, but in midsummer, the oxygen level may fall too low for coldwater fish. When this happens, the fish are forced into shallower water where they could die because of high temperatures.

In northern lakes, oxygen is depleted more rapidly in winter because the ice prevents replenishment by the wind. A blanket of snow or a layer of slush ice cuts off sunlight so plants do not produce oxygen through photosynthesis. Oxygen is still being consumed by aquatic organisms, so a shortage may soon develop, especially in eutrophic lakes. If snow or slush cover develops in early winter, the organisms may deplete all of the available oxygen before ice-out. Then the lake *winterkills*, or *freezes out*, (p. 25) and many of the fish die.

Some highly eutrophic lakes also undergo *summerkills* (p. 24). During a prolonged period of hot, still weather, heavy algae blooms develop. The algae produce oxygen by photosynthesis during the day, but consume huge quantities of oxygen by respiration at night. If there is no wind to add oxygen and circulate the epilimnion, nighttime fish kills may occur.

Another cause of summerkill is decomposition of aquatic plants at the end of the summer. When the plants die, bacteria active in the decomposition process consume enough oxygen to cause a short-term shortage. When oxygen levels fall too low, fish begin to show signs of stress. They often swim about slowly near the surface, where oxygen levels are highest, occasionally poking their snouts out of the water, as if gasping for air. If the oxygen shortage persists, however, fish begin to die.

OXYGEN is produced by aquatic plants through the process of photosynthesis. When sunlight strikes the chlorophyll in the plant's leaves, tiny oxygen bubbles are emitted as shown in this photo.

WINTERKILL becomes evident after the ice goes out in spring. If the oxygen level fell too low, and stayed low for more than a few days, almost all the fish die, with the exception of hardy species such as bullheads.

Understanding Oligotrophic Lakes

The low nutrient level in these lakes means that they produce little organic matter such as algae, invertebrates and fish.

Because there is such a small quantity of organic matter to decompose, the basins are slow to fill in with sediments. As a result, these lakes tend to be deep and cold, with high levels of oxygen all the way to the bottom.

The following diagram illustrates how the water temperature in a typical oligotrophic lake changes

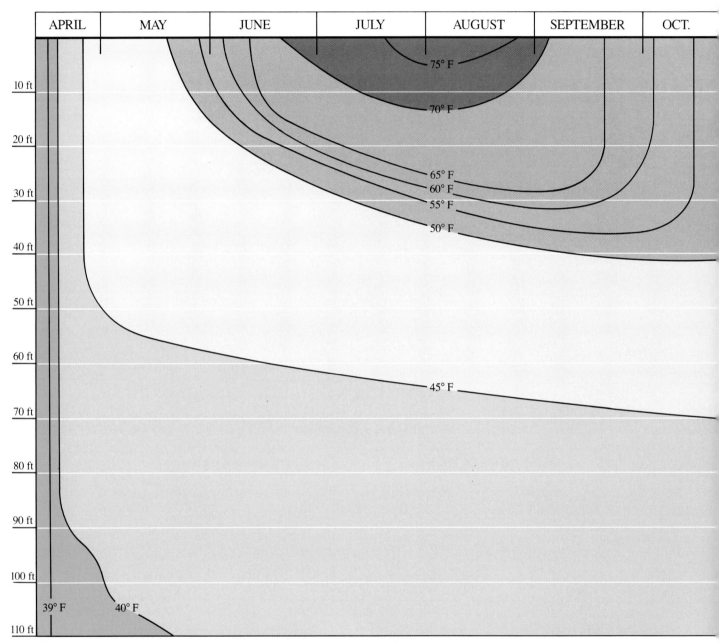

SPRING (mid-April through June). The ice goes out on April 15 and the surface soon warms to 39° F, the same as the bottom temperature. The spring turnover begins and the water mixes from top to bottom. Following the turnover, the shallows warm rapidly. By late June, the surface has reached the low 70s, but the temperature at 30 feet is only 49. The wind mixes the warmer, lighter water in the shallows, but the depths do not mix. Yet the oxygen level in the depths stays high because there is little decaying organic matter to consume it.

SUMMER (July through September). Gradual warming of the shallows continues until early August when the surface temperature peaks at 76° F. The depths continue to warm too, but at a much slower rate. In early June, the 50-degree temperature contour was at 17 feet; in late September, 41 feet. The bottom temperature remains at 43 through the summer. The shallows begin cooling rapidly in late August, and by late September, the surface temperature is 62. The oxygen level is still adequate from top to bottom.

from season to season, and how these changes affect fish location. Oxygen level is seldom a consideration in these lakes because the levels stay high at all depths throughout the year.

To compile this diagram, temperatures and oxygen levels were measured at a selected spot on the lake at weekly intervals throughout the year.

Temperature Key

under 40	40-45	46-50	51-60	61-70	71-80

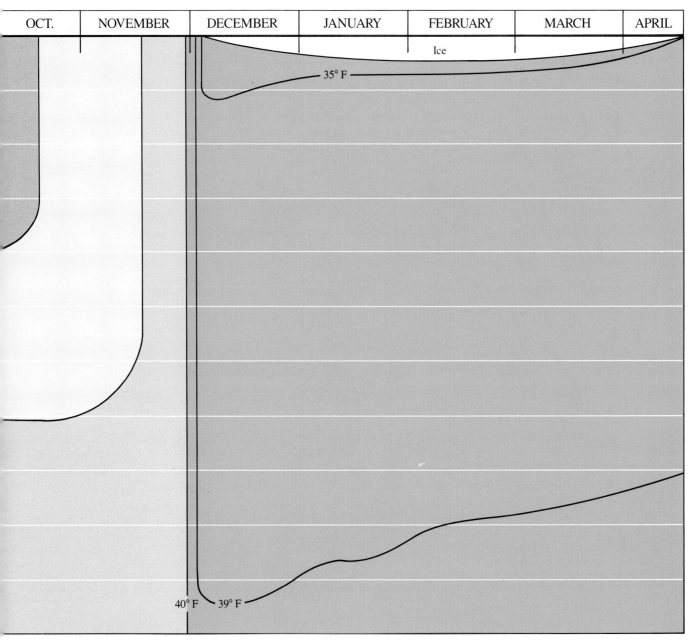

FALL (October to mid-December). As the surface continues to cool, the density of the shallow water begins to approach that of the deep water. With the strong density barrier to mixing removed, the wind can mix the water to a much greater depth. By late October, the water is a uniform 48° F from the surface to 70 feet and the fall turnover begins. The water continues to mix and cool until it reaches 39. The upper layers keep cooling even more, but the bottom temperature stabilizes. By early December, the surface temperature is 34; the bottom, still 39.

WINTER (mid-December to mid-April). The lake freezes up on December 10 and conditions under the ice remain quite stable through the winter season. The ice gradually thickens and is blanketed by a thick layer of snow, so very little sunlight can penetrate and practically no photosynthesis takes place. Nevertheless, the oxygen level remains high, even on the bottom. But as winter progresses, a strange phenomenon occurs: the deep water begins to warm slightly as a result of stored heat released from the bottom sediments.

Understanding Mesotrophic Lakes

Compared to oligotrophic lakes, mesotrophic lakes have more dissolved nutrients, so they produce more food and more fish. But they're generally shallower, so water temperatures in the depths during the summer are higher.

Because mesotrophic lakes have a greater quantity of organic material than oligotrophic lakes, dissolved oxygen is consumed at a faster rate. As a result, the depths are short of oxygen much of the year and cannot support fish.

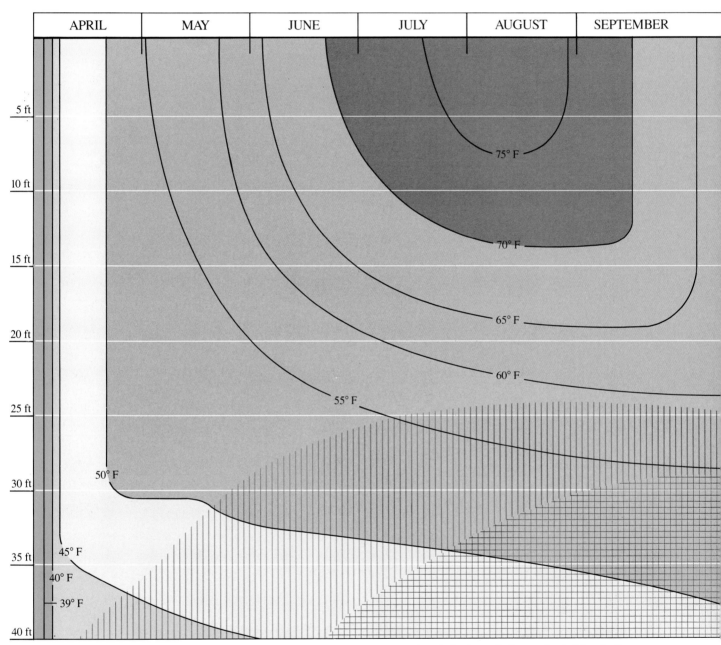

SPRING (April through June). The ice goes out April 1, and the surface soon warms to 39° F. The spring turnover begins and the water mixes from top to bottom. The shallows continue to warm, reaching 73 in late June, but the temperature in the depths lags behind, reaching only 46. During the turnover, the entire lake is saturated with oxygen, but after the turnover, oxygen in the depths is gradually used up. By late April, the oxygen level is marginal in water deeper than 35 feet; late May, 30 feet; and late June, 26 feet.

SUMMER (July through September). The shallows continue to warm even more, peaking at 78° F in late July, then gradually cooling to 64 by late September. As the summer progresses, the warm water penetrates to somewhat greater depths. In early July, the 70-degree contour is at 10 feet; by mid-September, 13 feet. During most of the summer, the oxygen level is marginal in water deeper than 25 feet. By late June, the oxygen level near the bottom is too low for gamefish to survive. This low-oxygen zone continues to expand through the summer.

The following diagram illustrates how the water temperature and oxygen level in a typical mesotrophic lake change from season to season, and how these changes affect fish location.

To compile this diagram, temperatures and oxygen levels were measured at a selected spot on the lake at weekly intervals throughout the year.

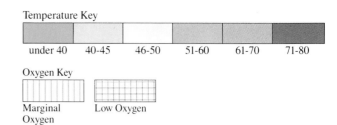

Temperature Key

under 40   40-45   46-50   51-60   61-70   71-80

Oxygen Key

Marginal Oxygen   Low Oxygen

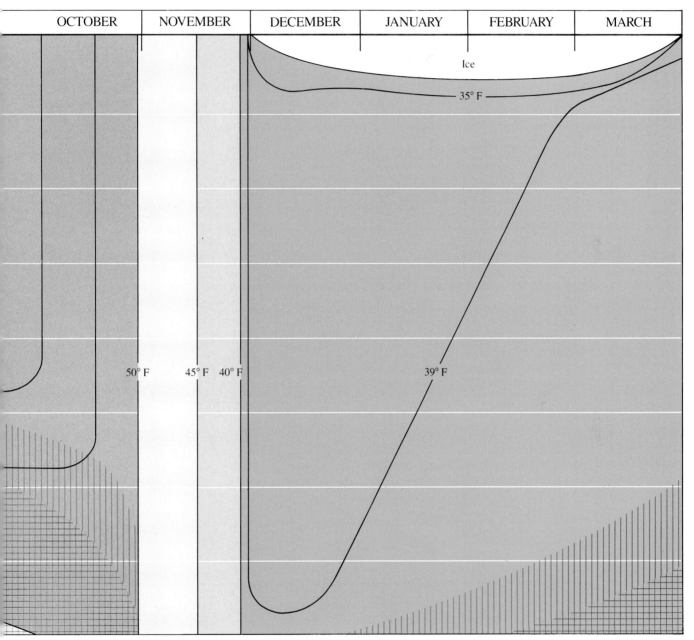

| OCTOBER | NOVEMBER | DECEMBER | JANUARY | FEBRUARY | MARCH |

Ice

35° F

50° F   45° F   40° F   39° F

FALL (October through December). The surface continues to cool and by late October reaches 50° F, the same as the bottom temperature. The fall turnover begins and the wind circulates the water from top to bottom. The cooling and mixing process continues for nearly a month. During the fall turnover, the lake is saturated with oxygen from top to bottom. By late November, the surface has cooled to 35, but the bottom temperature remains at 39, the temperature at which water is densest. The lake freezes over December 1.

WINTER (December through March). After freeze-up, temperature and oxygen levels remain stable until early January, but then the depths begin to warm as heat is released from the sediments. In early January, the 39-degree contour is at 33 feet; by late February, 5 feet. As winter progresses, the ice and snow cover thickens, preventing sunlight from penetrating to the depths. The oxygen level in the deep water begins to decline and by late March, is marginal below a depth of 30 feet. Near the bottom, there is no oxygen.

Understanding Eutrophic Lakes

Because these shallow, fertile lakes contain high levels of dissolved nutrients, they produce immense quantities of fish food and support large fish populations.

Living organisms and decaying organic matter consume oxygen at a very high rate, reducing the oxygen level in the depths and limiting where the fish can live in winter and possibly in summer.

The following diagram illustrates how the water temperature and oxygen level in a shallow eutrophic lake change from season to season, and how these

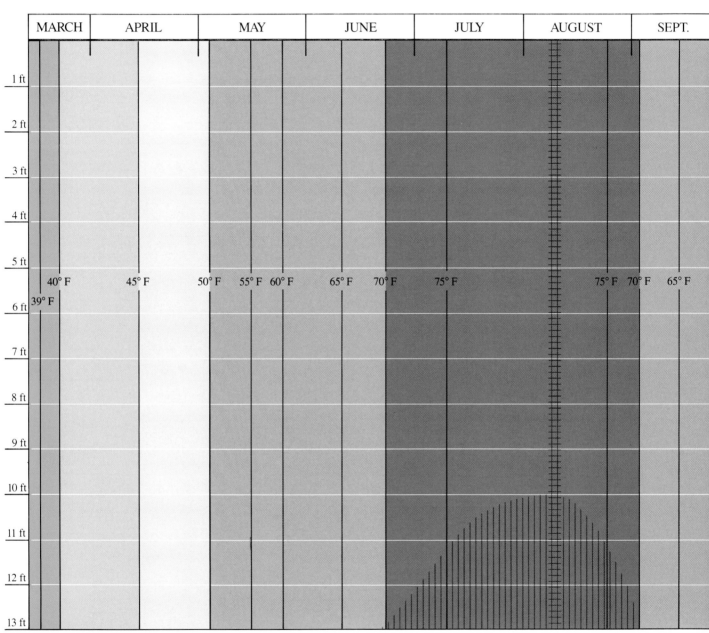

SPRING (mid-March to mid-June). After ice-out in mid-March, the water warms quickly to 39° F, and the lake mixes from top to bottom. The water continues to warm rapidly, and because the basin is so shallow, the wind continues to thoroughly mix the water; it's possible to find fish at any depth. But in mid-June, a marginal-oxygen zone begins to develop near the bottom. The warm water accelerates the rate at which organic matter in the bottom sediments decomposes, so oxygen is being consumed faster than it's replenished, even though the lake is still mixing.

SUMMER (mid-June through September). Warming and mixing continues until mid-July, when the water temperature reaches 82° F. The marginal-oxygen zone on the bottom continues to expand as oxygen is being consumed at an even faster rate. In early August, following a few days of hot, calm weather, an extremely heavy algae bloom develops. Then, on a still night, the algae consumes all of the oxygen from top to bottom. A summerkill results and many gamefish die. Most of the fish, though under severe stress for a short time, recover.

changes affect fish location. The lake depicted does not stratify in summer. Deeper eutrophic lakes form temperature layers in summer, much like the meso-trophic lake shown on pages 22 to 23.

To compile this diagram, temperatures and oxygen levels were measured at a selected spot on the lake at weekly intervals throughout the year.

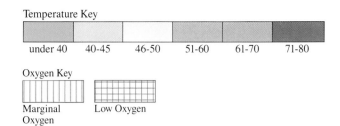

Temperature Key

| under 40 | 40-45 | 46-50 | 51-60 | 61-70 | 71-80 |

Oxygen Key

Marginal Oxygen   Low Oxygen

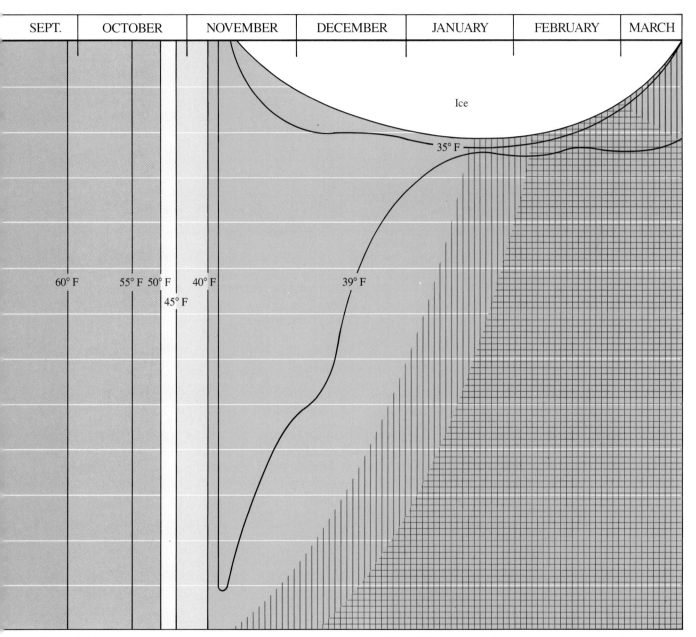

| SEPT. | OCTOBER | NOVEMBER | DECEMBER | JANUARY | FEBRUARY | MARCH |

Ice

35° F

60° F   55° F 50° F   40° F   39° F

45° F

FALL (October through December). As the water temperature drops, the rate of decomposition of the bottom sediments decreases; by mid-September, mixing restores adequate oxygen to all depths. The water continues to cool and mix uniformly from top to bottom. Then on a cold, still night in mid-November, the lake freezes up. Because there is no mixing by the wind once ice covers the surface, a zone of marginal oxygen begins to develop almost immediately, and within a few days, there is not enough oxygen on the bottom to support gamefish.

WINTER. (January through mid-March). As the ice and snow cover thickens, photosynthesis slows. At the same time, heat released from the sediments begins to warm the water. Oxygen is consumed by the bottom sediments much faster than it is produced, so the low-oxygen zone expands rapidly and fish are forced into shallower water. By early February, the entire lake is depleted of oxygen, causing an extensive winterkill. In early March, the ice cover thins, photosynthesis increases, and meltwater begins running into the lake, boosting the oxygen level.

How Wind Affects
Natural Lakes

Wind does much more than cause waves on a lake's surface. It has a dramatic effect on water temperature and clarity, it creates currents, and in large lakes, may even cause oscillations in the water level. The following wind-induced changes all have an impact on fish and fishing:

WAVE ACTION. A choppy surface scatters light rays, severely reducing the amount of light that penetrates to the depths. The bigger the waves, the more light penetration is reduced.

How wave action affects fishing depends mainly on water clarity. In clear lakes, wave action usually

improves fishing, especially in midday. Otherwise, the light is so bright that fish seek heavy cover, where they may be difficult to catch, or they go deep. But in murky lakes, wave action sometimes reduces the light level so much that fish cannot see well enough to feed.

WATER TEMPERATURE. In an average lake, about 90 percent of the sun's energy is absorbed in the upper 2 feet. On a sunny day, the surface warms rapidly, sometimes rising 15° F above the temperature of the water just below it.

Because the surface water is warmer and lighter, it resists mixing with the deeper water. As a result, it is easily blown along by the wind and accumulates on

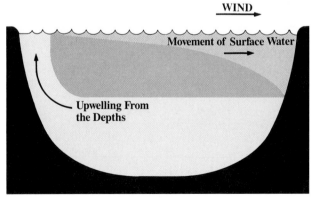

WIND

Movement of Surface Water

Upwelling From the Depths

Warm water collects on downwind shore; cool water on upwind

the downwind shore of the lake. At the same time, warm water is blown away from the upwind shore, so cold water from the depths wells up to replace it.

Waves scatter light rays, increasing gamefish activity

The temperature difference between the two shores may exceed 30° F.

Bays and inside turns in the breakline along the downwind shore often warm more than a straight shoreline;

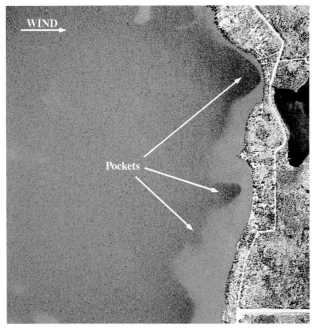
Pockets in the breakline collect warm water, drawing fish in spring

they trap the warm surface water and prevent it from mixing and cooling. Early in the season, when the main body of the lake is cold, these warmwater zones attract most species of gamefish.

CLARITY. In deep lakes, wind has little effect on the overall clarity. Because the lake is stratified, only the epilimnion circulates. However, the wind roils the water on shallow lips and points along the downwind

Mudlines are a tip-off to fast fishing

shore, creating a mudline. The reduced water clarity keeps the light level low enough that gamefish feed actively, even in midday.

The wind also spurs gamefish activity by blowing plankton toward the downwind shoreline. The thick layer of green, soupy water that sometimes results may look unappealing, but minnows move in to feed on the plankton, and the larger fish move in to feed on the minnows. The layer of plankton also helps filter out sunlight.

In a shallow, windswept lake, a strong wind can roil the water enough to greatly reduce the overall water clarity. The entire lake circulates, so silt stirred up from the bottom is mixed at all depths. After the wind subsides, it may take a week or more for the water to clear.

WIND-INDUCED CURRENTS. In large lakes, a sustained wind from the same direction may produce significant currents. The effects are most noticeable in narrows, between islands, under bridges, or any-place where the water funnels through a narrow

Narrows are a natural drawing card for gamefish

passage. The currents draw minnows, and gamefish soon follow.

SEICHES. Sustained winds in large lakes also produce *seiches*, oscillations in the water level. The wind, in effect, stacks up water on the downwind side of the lake and lowers the water on the upwind side. When the wind stops blowing, the water surface begins to rock, just as water in a bathtub rocks after you push it to one end. Gradually, the oscillations subside and the water level stabilizes.

Food

Where you find gamefish in natural lakes depends to a great extent on food. No matter if the water is too hot, too cold, too low in oxygen or too polluted, gamefish will move in if that's where the food is.

They may stay for only a short time, but they'll be there long enough to get a meal.

The importance of food in determining where and when to find fish is probably the least understood facet of fisheries science. The diet of gamefish in one lake often bears little resemblance to the diet of the same species of fish in a different lake.

For instance, walleyes in many lakes feed heavily on small yellow perch. The perch are structure-oriented, hanging on drop-offs around points and sunken islands. Consequently, that's where the walleyes will be. But in some lakes, walleyes rely more heavily on ciscoes, baitfish that often suspend in open water. Walleyes in these lakes spend much of their time cruising open reaches of the lake, far from any structure.

Even in the same lake, a fish's diet can change abruptly. Some walleye lakes, for example, have both perch and ciscoes. Walleyes typically feed on perch in spring and early summer, but in some lakes, they switch to ciscoes in midsummer.

Most anglers accustomed to fishing structure are lost when the fish are feeding in open water. And it's not

just walleyes that feed this way. So will northern pike, muskies, largemouth and smallmouth bass, crappies, and even bluegills, when the opportunity presents itself.

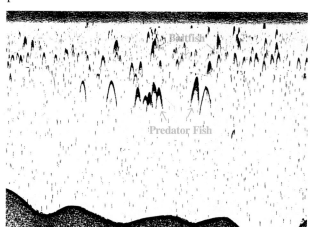

Suspended baitfish draw predators into open water

Circling, diving birds pinpoint feeding gamefish

But if you're aware of this feeding pattern and you own a good graph, you can scout expanses of open water, looking for schools of baitfish. Usually, the gamefish aren't far away.

Gulls and terns may also reveal the location of bait-fish schools. When you see the birds circling, diving and screeching, you can bet they've found a school of baitfish.

Even if you discover what the fish are eating and come up with a strategy for catching them, there's no guarantee that the pattern will last. A fish's diet can change overnight whenever there's an easy feeding opportunity.

For instance, gamefish will abandon their major food source during a heavy hatch of insects such as mayflies. Many fish feed almost exclusively on the nymphs that are rising toward the surface. The hatch generally takes place in the evening, so that's when the fish feed.

Even if it's the wrong time of day, you can tell if insects have been hatching by looking for the skins littering the surface. Sometimes they're so thick they form windrows.

Shed skins mean there's been a recent insect hatch

What the fish are eating influences not only when and where you fish, but what you use for bait. A fish feeding on mayflies, for example, would pay no attention to a minnow plug, but would probably take a small, drab-colored jig.

There's been a great deal written about the importance of checking the stomach contents of your fish.

But if you're not catching fish, you have no stomachs to check. And if you're catching a lot of fish, you already know when and where to get them and what they're biting on.

If you catch a straggler, however, a look at its stomach contents may suggest how you can catch more. If you don't mind digging through a pail of fish innards, you can gather some valuable information at the fish-cleaning shack.

A belly full of small perch means minnows would be good bait

Not only does the type of food affect how fish behave, so does the quantity. In a eutrophic lake teeming with forage fish, for instance, a largemouth bass may feed for only a half-hour or so each day. It can easily eat its fill in that time, and doesn't have to feed again until the following day. But in a mesotrophic lake with a sparser forage crop, a largemouth must spend more time searching for food, so the feeding period lasts longer.

Of course, the quantity of food also affects how many fish a lake can produce. In any lake, plankton is the foundation of the food chain. A eutrophic lake may produce 10 times as much plankton as a mesotrophic lake of the same size. As a result, it will produce 10 times as much food and 10 times as many pounds of fish (see chart below).

Food and Fish Production in Different Lake Types

	Plankton (pounds per acre)	Invertebrates (pounds per acre)	Baitfish (pounds per acre)	Predator Fish (pounds per acre)
Eutrophic lakes	20,000	2,000	200	20
Mesotrophic lakes	5,000	500	50	5
Oligotrophic lakes	1,000	100	10	1

Common Foods for Gamefish in Natural Lakes

ZOOPLANKTON. These tiny animals make up the bulk of the diet of many baitfish; they're also eaten by juvenile gamefish.

YELLOW PERCH. Young-of-the-year perch are an important food for almost all predator fish in shallow to mid-depth northern lakes.

LARVAL INSECTS. A staple for panfish and young gamefish of all kinds. Adult walleyes and bass may gorge themselves on large nymphs.

YOUNG SUNFISH. A common food for predator fish, especially largemouth bass, in shallow, weedy lakes.

ADULT INSECTS. While less important than larval forms, adult insects are commonly eaten by surface-feeding bass, panfish and salmonids.

SHAD. A mainstay in the diet of most gamefish in oxbows and other lakes connected to large rivers, especially in the South.

SMELT. These invaders from the sea make good forage in deep, cold lakes, but they sometimes eat small gamefish.

BULLHEADS. A major food item for largemouth bass, stocked walleyes and other predator fish in periodic freeze-out lakes.

CISCOES. The most common deep-water forage fish in deep, cool lakes around the Great Lakes and throughout central Canada.

SMALL CRUSTACEANS. Tiny shrimp, scuds and other small crustaceans are a major food item for panfish and young gamefish.

SHINERS. More than 100 species of these small baitfish exist. They're eaten by nearly all gamefish in natural lakes of all types.

CRAYFISH. This large crustacean is a favorite of largemouth bass, smallmouth bass and yellow perch in all types of natural lakes.

BASIC TYPES of aquatic vegetation are shown in the above photo. The (1) *emergent* vegetation protrudes well above the surface. The (2) *floating-leaved* vegetation rests on the surface. The (3) *submerged* vegetation is completely below the surface, with the exception of the flowering heads, which may protrude slightly.

Aquatic Vegetation

Besides enriching the water with oxygen, aquatic plants are the number one source of cover for gamefish in most natural lakes. Because the water level fluctuates very little, natural lakes do not have the flooded trees and brush so important as cover in man-made lakes.

Small fish hide among aquatic plants to escape predators. Larger fish use the plants for shade and ambush cover. If the plants form a dense enough canopy, they will keep the water underneath a few degrees cooler than the surrounding water. Aquatic plants also attract a variety of crustaceans, baitfish and larval insects, all prime gamefish foods.

Gamefish will use whatever kind of aquatic plant that's available, but most fish prefer broad-leaved plants or plants that form dense mats, rather than narrowleaf plants or those that grow in sparse stands. The broad leaves and dense mats provide more shade and ambush cover for adult fish, more escape cover for juvenile fish and baitfish, and more surface area to which larval insects can attach.

In most cases, you'll find more gamefish along the edge of the weeds than deep within a thick weedbed.

How Gamefish Use Aquatic Vegetation

ESCAPE COVER. Young fish hide beneath floating-leaved plants or alongside submerged plants to escape larger fish, birds and even predaceous insects.

AMBUSH COVER. Predator fish lie among submerged plants or thick stands of emergents to hide from baitfish or other types of prey.

FOOD. Aquatic plants harbor foods such as baitfish, crustaceans and larval aquatic insects, which often cling to or burrow into the stems and leaves.

SHADE. Floating-leaved plants or dense mats of submerged plants block out most sunlight, creating a darker, cooler environment for fish.

Large predator fish cannot maneuver through dense weeds as easily as small baitfish, so they have trouble feeding. They're better off hiding along the edge of the weeds, where they can easily dart out to grab an unsuspecting baitfish.

Very shallow lakes may have weeds growing everywhere, so there is no distinct edge. But in deeper lakes, weeds are usually confined to a definite band. All plants require sunlight, so the maximum depth to which they grow depends mainly on water clarity.

Some kinds of plants can grow deeper than others because of differences in the amount of light necessary for photosynthesis. For instance, photosynthesis in hydrilla takes place at a low light level; in clear water, the plant can grow to a depth of 50 feet.

Because gamefish tend to concentrate along the edge of the deepest-growing weeds, or the *outside weedline*, the exact depth at which it forms is important for anglers to know (see below).

In the North, many lakes have a weedless zone along shore, the result of winter ice cover or wave action. Because the shallows freeze all the way to the bottom, weeds are less likely to take root there. And even if they do, wave action may rip them loose, especially if the bottom is hard enough that the root system is shallow. With no plants in the shallows, the deeper weeds have a distinct *inside weedline*, which can attract just as many fish as the outside weedline.

The chart at right describes many of the common kinds of aquatic plants found in natural lakes and explains where they are likely to grow.

Inside vs. Outside Weedline

INSIDE WEEDLINES form at depths of 2 to 4 feet, depending on ice thickness and wave action. On a gradually tapering shoreline, the weedline may be more than 100 feet from shore; on a steeper shoreline, only 10 feet.

OUTSIDE WEEDLINES form at various depths, depending on water clarity. In a turbid lake, the outside weedline may form at a depth of less than 5 feet; in a very clear lake, at 20 feet or more.

Common Aquatic Plants in Natural Lakes

BULRUSHES. Tough-stemmed plants growing to a depth of 6 feet, usually on a sandy bottom in an area with good water circulation.

HYDRILLA. This invader of southern lakes is found on mucky bottoms. It needs little light, so it grows to depths of 50 feet.

CATTAILS. Dense stands grow in quiet waters usually no more than 3 feet deep; generally found on soft, mucky bottoms.

COONTAIL. Found in all types of natural lakes, coontail forms thick mats on bottoms ranging from muck to sand to gravel.

MAIDENCANE. Grassy plant growing on a sandy bottom, usually in depths of 2 feet or less. Mats may break away and float freely.

MILFOIL. Resembles coontail, but its leaflets are branched, much like the vanes of a feather. It usually grows on a muddy bottom.

WILD RICE. Grows in clear water less than 3 feet deep with a mucky bottom. The plants lie flat at first, then stand up when mature.

BLADDERWORT. Often found in sheltered bays of deep, cold lakes, bladderwort generally grows on a soft, muddy bottom.

LILY PADS. Found in shallow, mucky bays in all types of natural lakes; leaves of various species range from 2 to 18 inches across.

CABBAGE. Normally found on a firm bottom; some varieties grow to the surface out of water more than 10 feet deep.

WATER HYACINTH. Another invader of southern lakes, hyacinth forms free-floating colonies that move about with the wind.

SANDGRASS. Also called muskgrass because of its skunky odor; dense mats grow to depths of 35 feet on bottoms of sand or fine gravel.

POWER PLANTS that burn coal are a major cause of acid rain. Although stiffer environmental laws now require many plants to install *scrubbers* to remove sulfur dioxide, acid rain continues to be a serious problem.

Threats to Natural Lakes

Human activities create a myriad of problems for natural lakes. Some of the more obvious ones, such as chemical pollution, get the most publicity, but others that we seldom hear about are no less serious. Following are some of the major threats:

SHORELINE DEVELOPMENT. To create clean sandy beaches, lakeshore property owners often remove aquatic vegetation and sometimes even haul

Clean sand beaches mean no spawning areas

in sand, covering rocky shorelines that provide valuable spawning habitat for gamefish.

Another problem: to firm up the ground for residential or commercial purposes, developers frequently deposit huge quantities of fill in marshlands adjacent to natural lakes. Although these marshes are seemingly unimportant, many species of fish use them as spawning areas in spring and nursery areas in summer. If too much marshland or shoreline is filled in, or too many aquatic plants removed, gamefish populations suffer.

MAN-MADE EUTROPHICATION. Municipal and agricultural wastes, lawn fertilizers and other nutrients find their way into lakes, causing nuisance algae blooms or heavy weed growth that chokes off

Runoff from feedlots and farm fields increases nutrient levels

parts of the shallows. The weeds make fishing almost impossible and interfere with navigation.

If the water becomes too fertile, winterkill or summerkill may result. Gamefish disappear and only species tolerant of low oxygen levels, such as bullheads, can survive.

In some areas, natural resources agencies have installed aeration systems that replenish oxygen and prevent winterkill.

ACID RAIN. Emissions from coal-burning power plants and automobiles are converted to acids in the atmosphere and the wind carries them far from their source. When it rains, the acid falls to earth, often hundreds of miles away.

If enough acid rain falls on or washes into a poorly buffered lake, the acidity of the water increases. If the pH drops below 6.0, it starts to impair gamefish reproduction. Acid rain is rarely a problem in lakes with moderate to high fertility levels. These lakes contain enough buffer to neutralize the acid.

TOXIC CHEMICALS. Although government regulations now prohibit practically all direct discharge of toxic chemicals into lakes, the fish in many natural lakes contain significant levels of toxic substances such as mercury or PCBs. For health reasons, anglers are advised to limit consumption of certain gamefish from these waters.

In some cases, trace levels of these chemicals remain from the days when they were discharged. But in other cases, scientists are not sure where the chemicals came from. PCBs, for instance, have been found in lakes in remote regions of Canada, far from any known discharge point. The only explanation is that they came down in the rain.

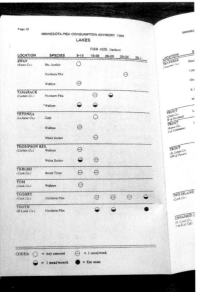

Many states publish fish-consumption advisories

OVERFISHING. Not only are there more anglers today than ever before, but they have better equipment and more fishing expertise.

Consequently, many lakes are being over-harvested. The first symptom of the problem is a noticeable decline in the size of the fish. Anglers catch them before they can grow to an acceptable size.

To combat the problem, many natural resources agencies have adopted regulations to control the size of fish anglers harvest. *Slot limits*, for instance, allow anglers to keep small fish and large fish, but require them to release

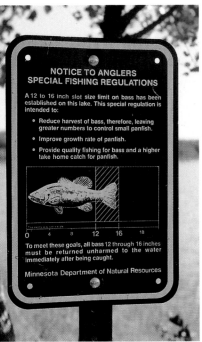

Expect to see more and more special regulations to prevent overharvest

medium-sized fish. This type of regulation is gaining popularity because anglers can take the eating-sized fish, and any trophy they might catch. The medium-sized fish, including the bulk of the spawners, are released to reproduce and grow.

EXOTICS. Non-native fishes, crustaceans and even mollusks are showing up at an ever increasing rate, especially around the Great Lakes region. The white perch, for instance, previously found only along the Eastern Seaboard, is now established throughout the Great Lakes. It threatens to spread to connecting waters and could compete with native panfishes.

The European ruffe and the zebra mussel were brought into the Great Lakes in the bilges of foreign ships. The ruffe, a small perchlike fish, has an extremely high reproductive capacity and could also compete with native panfishes. The zebra mussel, a tiny clam, firmly attaches itself to boat bottoms, buoys and rocks. Some scientists are concerned that dense colonies will smother spawning reefs and filter out plankton needed by small fishes.

Exotic plants have created major problems in many parts of the country. Once introduced into a lake, they grow at an astounding rate, often crowding out

Unwelcome invaders include (1) the European ruffe, (2) the zebra mussel and (3) Eurasian milfoil

native plants and clogging channels and bays to the point where they're no longer navigable. Hydrilla and water hyacinth have long been a problem in the South, and Eurasian milfoil is spreading at an alarming rate throughout much of the country.

How to Fish Natural Lakes

Lakes of the Far North

Every fisherman has dreamed of tangling with giant lake trout and pike in these pristine lakes

Lakes of the Far North are an angler's paradise. Not only do they offer unequaled fishing, but in summer, die-hards can fish practically nonstop because of the long days.

Most lakes of this type lie in the Northwest Territories. They can be divided into arctic and subarctic lakes. Arctic lakes lie above the tree line; subarctic lakes, in a zone extending about 500 miles to the south.

Arctic lakes generally open up in July and freeze in September. The surface temperatures may never rise above 50° F, and the prime fishing season lasts only six weeks. On most subarctic lakes, the ice goes out sometime in June, and they freeze up in October. The majority of arctic and subarctic lakes have very low fertility, with total phosphorus levels (p. 17) of 5 parts per billion or less.

Owing to the short fishing season and the remote location of these lakes, some of them have seldom, if ever, been fished. There's so much water that natural resource agencies cannot even provide an accurate estimate of the number of lakes, let alone detailed information on specific lakes.

These lakes are famed for their huge lake trout and northern pike. The world-record laker, 65 pounds, was caught in Great Bear Lake, NWT, in 1970, and lakers weighing over 50 pounds are taken each year. Lake Athabasca in northern Saskatchewan yielded a 102-pound laker to commercial gill-netters in 1961. The Canadian record pike, 42 pounds 12 ounces, was caught in Lake Athabasca in 1954, but there have been reports of considerably larger pike, up to 55 pounds.

Some lakes of the Far North also support Arctic grayling, although most grayling live in connecting streams, rather than in the lakes themselves. Arctic char make seasonal runs into many lakes connected to the Arctic Ocean and, in some cases, become landlocked. Whitefish, though ignored by most fishermen, are found in practically all lakes of the Far North. They're gaining popularity because they rise to a fly and are excellent eating. Walleyes inhabit some of the warmer, shallower lakes of the subarctic region.

There is little, if any, ice fishing on most of these lakes because wintertime air temperatures are so cold and the ice thickness is so great. Temperatures in the -40 to -60° F range are not uncommon. Subarctic lakes generally have 4 to 6 feet of ice; arctic lakes, 7 or 8. Snow depths average about 3 feet.

Because of the cold, infertile water in these lakes, food is scarce and growth rates of fish very slow.

Even as far south as northern Saskatchewan, the growth rate of lake trout averages only ½ pound per year.

Gamefish in these lakes reach large size only because they live so long. Aging studies conducted by Canadian biologists reveal that lake trout may live as long as 67 years. Northern pike sometimes live 25 years or more. In the southern portion of their range, these species seldom live half that long.

This slow growth rate means that these lakes produce far fewer pounds of fish per year than similar lakes farther south. Typically, they yield only about 5 pounds of fish per acre per year. A farm-country lake in the Midwest might produce 500 pounds or more.

With productivity this low, lakes of the Far North cannot hold up under catch-and-keep regulations. To preserve fishing quality in their lakes, many lodges and camps have imposed their own regulations, allowing guests to keep only one trophy-sized fish, or in some cases, none at all. Small fish may be kept for shore lunches.

Anglers interested in trophies should check to see if the lake they're planning to fish has been commercially netted in recent years. If it has, the chances of catching a real trophy are considerably less.

Case Study:

Selwyn Lake, Saskatchewan & Northwest Territories

Selwyn Lake is one of Canada's best-kept secrets. Although the lake and its fishery bear many similarities to other more famous lakes in the same region, like Nueltin and Kasba, it sees only a handful of anglers each year.

Tent camp on Selwyn Lake operated by Far North Recreation

Located along the boundary of Saskatchewan and the Northwest Territories, this 135,000-acre body of water has only two small fishing camps. There was a small amount of commercial netting by the native Chipewayan Indians in the 1980s, but the remote location of the lake made the operation economically unfeasible. Besides a minor amount of angling in the vicinity of the camps and a little subsistence netting by Indians, there is no other fishing.

The lake is fed by dozens of small streams. The outlet, the Porcupine River, flows from the southeast end of Porcupine Bay.

Like most lakes of this type, Selwyn is dominated by lake trout and northern pike, many of which reach trophy size. The Porcupine River has an excellent population of Arctic grayling, but few grayling inhabit the lake itself.

The Selwyn Lake vicinity experiences the widest temperature variation on the North American continent. Daytime summer temperatures are usually in the 70s but occasionally reach 95. In winter, temperatures in the -30 to -40° F range are common, and occasionally the mercury plunges to -60. The ice, which gets 4 to 5 feet thick, normally goes out in

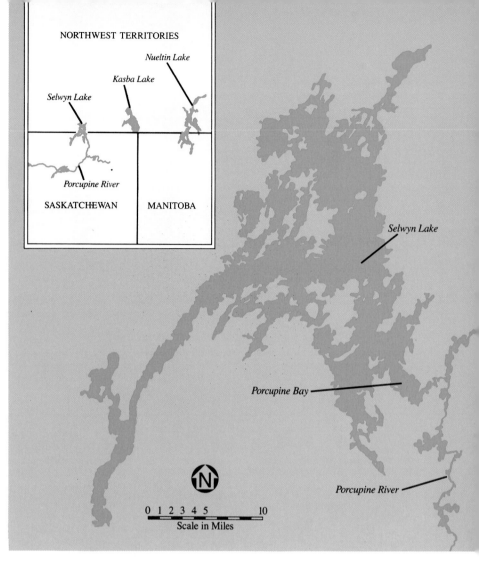

the first week of June, and the lake freezes up again in mid-October.

Selwyn Lake has never been surveyed, so there is no exact information on its physical makeup. Anglers, however, have reported depths exceeding 300 feet.

In an average year, the surface temperature in the main lake is about 47° F on July 1, 64 on August 1, and 55 on September 1. The bays warm faster than the main lake the first half of the season, but cool faster the second half.

Even with surface temperatures so low, there is a distinct thermocline from mid-July through August because the deep water is so cold. Below 50 feet, for instance, the temperature is around 45° F most of the summer.

The lake, which lies on the Canadian Shield, is surrounded by rugged terrain with numerous rocky outcrops mixed with areas of bog and muskeg and stands of small black spruce. The lake bottom is just as rugged, with hundreds of islands and shallow reefs next to water more than 100 feet deep.

Although the main body of the lake has almost no aquatic vegetation, the shallower bays have a fair amount, including lily pads, cabbage, bladderwort and sedge.

The water is very clear. Although no Secchi disk reading is available, you can see a white lure 15 to 20 feet down. The water level remains quite stable from year to year, seldom varying more than a foot.

Because of the light fishing pressure, there is no overharvest problem in Selwyn Lake at present. But camp operators encourage anglers to release the large fish and keep only a few small ones for food. This way, Selwyn Lake will continue to be one of Canada's premier trophy lakes far into the future.

Selwyn Lake Physical Data

Acreage	135,000
Average depth	unknown
Maximum depth	over 300 ft
Clarity	20 ft
Color	clear
Total phosphorus (parts per billion)	unknown
Limits of thermocline	22 to 38 ft
Average date of freeze-up	mid-October
Average date of ice-out	early June

Selwyn Lake Habitat (*sample locations of habitats are numbered on satellite photo*)

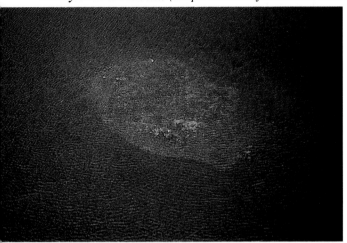

1. ROCKY REEFS that top off at 10 feet or less are good lake trout spawning areas. You'll find lakers on the reefs starting about mid-August.

2. BAYS hold northerns all year. The fish spawn far back in the bay, then move farther out as the water warms. Some bays also draw lakers in early summer.

3. INLET STREAMS carry in warmer water, so they draw spawning runs of northern pike in spring. They hold grayling throughout the year.

4. EXTENSIONS from islands and points are prime lake trout feeding areas. The fish feed on top of the shelf in morning and evening, and rest off the edge in midday.

5. SLICKS, sections of smooth water just above the rapids, hold grayling and lake trout when the water is high and the rapids are too turbulent.

6. RAPIDS are key spots for grayling at low and normal water stages. They lie behind the large rocks, then dart out to grab drifting insects.

Landsat Photograph →

Selwyn Lake:

Lake Trout

To catch lakers in the Far North, forget most of what you know about catching them farther south. Because of the cold climate, the surface temperature remains in the lake trout's comfort range during much of the

open-water season. So you can catch them in relatively shallow water all summer.

When the ice goes out in early June, lakers begin cruising the shallows to find food. You'll find them on shallow reefs, generally at depths of 20 feet or less, in bays and along practically any shoreline.

In early season, most anglers simply troll the shallows with good-sized spoons. There's always the chance of catching a 30-pound-plus laker in Selwyn, but that doesn't mean you need heavy tackle. A medium- to medium-heavy-power spinning or baitcasting outfit spooled with 10- to 15-pound mono is ideal. Attach your spoon with a ball-bearing swivel to minimize line twist. You'll have more fun catching lakers on lighter tackle, and you'll seldom lose a fish because you're fighting them in open water where there are no obstructions.

Trout are remarkably easy to catch in Selwyn; it's not unusual to take 50 a day, with most in the 4- to 12-pound class. The big trout, those weighing over 20 pounds, are harder to come by, probably because they're feeding on forage fish considerably larger than the lures most anglers use.

The small trout feed primarily on 4- to 5-inch ciscoes, but the big ones prefer larger fish, such as suckers, whitefish, burbot and young lake trout. They won't hesitate to take a fish weighing 2 or 3 pounds.

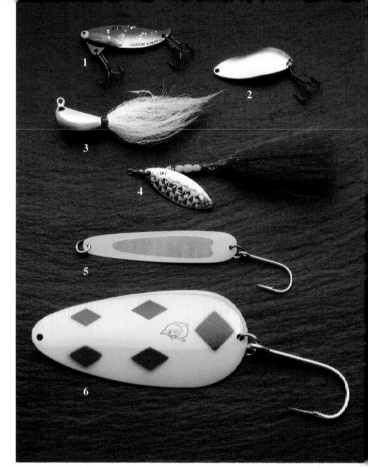

LURES for lake trout include: (1) ½-ounce Heddon Sonar, (2) Acme Little Cleo, (3) 1-ounce bucktail jig, (4) Mepps Aglia Long spinner, (5) Luhr-Jensen Flutter Spoon, (6) Eppinger Huskie-Devle.

Lakers eat fish as small as ciscoes (inset) or as big as this 2-pound lake trout

Trout are basically homebodies, seldom venturing more than a mile or two from their usual open-lake hangouts. But on Selwyn and many other lakes of the Far North, some trout move into shallow bays in early season. The bays are warmer than the main lake, so they draw huge schools of baitfish, mainly

ciscoes. Most of the trout in the bays run 4 to 8 pounds; seldom will you catch a big one. The larger trout seem to prefer colder temperatures and lower light levels, so they stay closer to the deep water.

Not all shallow bays draw trout, but Arctic terns will show you which ones do. The birds can easily spot the cisco schools in the clear water. While the terns divebomb the baitfish from above, the trout grab them from below. Using a light spinning outfit with 6- or 8-pound mono, cast a small spoon or spinner into the area the birds are working. You'll catch a trout on almost every cast.

By late July, most of the trout in the bays have moved to the main lake. There, the surface water has warmed to the low 60s, the high end of the lake trout's comfort range. Small trout will tolerate these temperatures, and some of them remain in the shallows. But most go deeper. To reach their preferred temperature range, about 50° F, they need only to descend to about 30 feet. The majority of the fish, however, including most of the big ones, go deeper yet, from 50 to 70 feet.

You can catch trout almost anywhere with sufficient depth, but you'll find the largest concentrations around major food shelves. An island or point with a large, shallow reef extending from it will hold more trout than an island or point that drops off sharply all around. Trout spend most of the day along the reef's breakline, and some of them will move up on the reef to feed in overcast weather or in the evening.

Trolling works just as well in summer as in spring; fishermen simply add more weight as the trout go deeper. If you know where there's a school, however, you'll do better if you hover over the fish and jig vertically with a vibrating blade or bucktail jig. An LCR is a big help for this type of fishing. Portable models with transducers mounted on suction cups are ideal for bush-country fishing.

If the fish are deep but not really concentrated, use wire line or portable downriggers. A good wire-line rig consists of a stiff 6-foot trolling rod with a roller guide on the tip, a sturdy baitcasting reel, and single-strand stainless-steel line, about 20-pound test.

Using either a Bait-Walker or three-way swivel rig, attach a 6-foot leader of 15-pound mono and tie on a thin, bright-colored spoon. Simply lower the weight (most anglers use 8 to 12 ounces) to bottom and troll slowly along the break.

Portable downriggers are perfect for these remote lakes. They're light and compact, yet with a 3- to 5-pound cannonball, you can troll at depths exceeding 75 feet. Even if the trout are suspended, it's easy to keep your lure at the precise depth. And when you hook a fish, you can fight it on light tackle with no heavy weight on the line to detract from the sport.

A Portable Backcountry Downrigger System

ATTACH a portable downrigger to the gunwale of your boat. Some models can be fastened securely by tightening a single knob.

TAPE a piece of PVC pipe to a seat strut if you need an extra rod holder. The struts on most boats are inclined at about the right angle.

RIG your LCR in a box such as those used for ice fishing. A motorcycle battery provides enough power for several days of fishing.

FASTEN your transducer to a 1 × 4 and clamp the board to your transom. Make sure the transducer is at the proper height and angle.

CLIP your line into a release on or just above a 3- to 5-pound weight. With the type of release shown, remember to twist your line about six times.

LOWER the weight to the right depth and begin trolling. Watch your LCR closely and be ready to crank up the weight if the water gets shallower.

You can catch lakers on practically any spoon, spinner, plug, jig or vibrating blade. But big lures improve your odds of catching big trout.

Remember that a laker weighing 20 pounds or more can easily eat a 2- to 3-pound fish.

In most lake trout waters, fly-fishermen seldom have a chance at lakers because they're too deep. But in Selwyn and other

Lakers love colorful streamers

lakes of the Far North, you can take them on flies in tributaries and outlet streams, when they're on the shallow food shelves or when they're chasing ciscoes in the bays. Use a 7-weight fly rod with a sink-tip line and a 2- to 3-inch, bright-colored streamer.

As fall approaches, your chances of catching big lakers improves. Starting in mid-August, the spawners begin to concentrate on shallow, rocky reefs or on rocky shelves extending from the main shoreline or islands. You can catch them using the same shallow-water techniques as in spring.

Lakers bite anytime of day, but most of the big ones are caught in morning or early evening. The action slows when the sun goes down. Overcast days with a slight chop are better than calm, sunny days.

Tips for Catching Lake Trout

CAST to any swirl you see on the surface. Lake trout feed on ciscoes and insects in the shallows, especially in the evening. The fish are quite aggressive, so they'll bite on practically anything you toss out.

LOOK for swarming, diving terns; they often pinpoint schools of lake trout feeding on ciscoes. When you find the birds, you'll have a tough time making a cast without catching a trout.

RELEASE a trout without boating it by grabbing the hook with a longnose pliers, then giving it a sharp twist. Use barbless hooks; they come out more easily, so they won't injure fish you intend to release.

Selwyn Lake:

Northern Pike

On Selwyn Lake, a 20-pound pike barely rates a mention. When conditions are right, you might catch several that size in a day. Although there are no authenticated angling records for Selwyn, pike over 40 pounds have been reported.

Pike spend practically all of their time in shallow bays off the main lake. Bays that have expanses of water less than 10 feet deep, along with some deeper water, hold the most pike. You'll find considerably fewer pike in bays with shorelines that slope rapidly into deep water. Some pike bays have lily pads or submerged vegetation such as cabbage or bladderwort, but other equally good bays have almost no vegetation.

Pike spawn in the bays and adjoining marshes in late May and early June. Fishing is usually slow for the first week or two following ice-out, although you may catch a few males. The larger females are still recuperating from spawning and haven't started to feed. The action picks up in late June as the pike begin gorging themselves on suckers, burbot, ciscoes, and lake trout that are chasing the ciscoes. A surprising number of trout caught in the bays show scars from pike bites.

Pike concentrate in the back ends of the bays, where the water is warmest and baitfish most plentiful. But during hot weather or on sunny days, they move closer to the mouths of the bays or into deeper channels within the bays. In August, look for big pike in deep cabbage beds near bay entrances. A few stragglers also hang around rocky points near the mouths of bays or in the main lake.

To cast heavy pike lures and set the hook in a pike's bony mouth, you'll need a heavy baitcasting outfit. A stiff 6- to 7-foot rod and a beefy level-wind reel with a high gear ratio are ideal. You can use 20-pound mono, but you'll get a better hook set with 30- to 40-pound Dacron because it doesn't stretch. Always use a steel leader, preferably one made of solid wire. Many of these pike have never seen a lure, so there's no need for finesse.

Any big, flashy lure will work, but a bucktail is the most consistent producer. As you drift or motor along the bank, cast the lure as close to shore as possible and reel steadily. Watch closely as the lure approaches the boat; often, there's a pike right behind it. If so, reel the lure to within a foot of the rod tip, plunge the rod into the water, and start figure-eighting.

LURES for northern pike include: (1) 1-ounce pyramid jig with Reapertail, (2) Bomber Long-A Magnum, (3) Mepps Giant Killer Tandem, (4) Bagley DB-06, and (5) Eppinger Huskie-Jr.

If the pike is interested, it will make a swipe at the lure within seconds. If it misses, it may drop back momentarily, but will probably make another pass at the lure. If the pike follows several feet behind the lure and keeps its distance while you figure-eight, reel up and resume casting; there's little chance it will strike.

Despite their aggressive nature, Selwyn Lake pike are moody. One day, they'll hit almost anything you throw at them; the next, they'll follow your bait but refuse to strike. In spring, they bite best on calm, sunny afternoons, but during the rest of the year, overcast, breezy days are better.

RELEASE any big pike you don't want for a trophy. Because they're so aggressive, pike are extremely vulnerable to overfishing.

Where to Find Pike

BACK ENDS of bays warm soonest, so they draw pike in spring and early summer. The shallower the water and muckier the bottom, the sooner the water will warm.

OVERFLOWS from nearby lakes cause dense weed growth, which draws pike in midsummer. You can see where overflows enter by looking for a band of light green trees.

ROCKY REEFS in large bays attract baitfish, which in turn attract pike. The reefs are most productive when they're exposed to the wind.

SEDGES hold northern pike until midsummer. Often the fish are so far back into the grass that casting to them is almost impossible.

Selwyn Lake:
Arctic Grayling

Dubbed "sailfish of the North" for their oversized dorsal fin, Arctic grayling are great acrobats. When hooked, they sometimes clear the water by 3 feet.

Although few grayling inhabit the main body of Selwyn Lake, there are plenty of them in the inlet streams and in the outlet, the Porcupine River. Grayling prefer fast water, so you'll find most of them around rapids. They run 1 to 2 pounds, with a few over 3.

Spawning begins in late May or early June, often when ice still remains on the lake. Grayling deposit their eggs on clean beds of gravel or small rock near the rapids, but unlike stream trout, do not build redds. During the spawning period, they're not likely to hit flies or fast-moving lures, but they'll take a $\frac{1}{16}$- to $\frac{1}{32}$-ounce dark-colored jig. Using an ultralight spinning outfit and 4-pound mono, cast across stream, keeping your rod tip high and your line tight as the current washes the jig over the gravel or rocks. If you have trouble detecting strikes, attach a small bobber.

After grayling finish spawning in late June, look for them behind large rocks, below points or indentations in the shoreline or beneath undercut banks. You'll also find them in the slicks just above the rapids. Most anglers simply use spinners or small spoons, quartering their casts upstream, then reeling just fast enough that the lure occasionally bumps bottom.

Fly casting offers the most excitement. Grayling aren't fussy; they'll take a variety of dry flies, nymphs or small streamers. Use a 5-weight fly rod, floating line, and a 4-pound leader. When you hook a fish, play it carefully; a scrappy grayling can easily snap a light tippet in fast water.

LURES include: (1) Mepps Aglia spinner, (2) K.O. Wobbler, (3) Wooly Bugger, (4) Mickey Finn, (5) Black Gnat, (6) $\frac{1}{32}$-ounce jig, (7) bobber rig with $\frac{1}{32}$-ounce jig.

"Two-Story" Lakes

*You've got a choice of warmwater or coldwater
fish in these "two-in-one" lakes*

Two-story lakes, also called *combination* lakes, are thermally stratified bodies of water that support warmwater fish in the shallows and coldwater fish in the depths. In order for coldwater fish to survive, the lake must have a good supply of oxygen in the depths year around.

The majority of two-story lakes are ice-scour lakes (p. 9), formed when glaciers scraped away the topsoil overlying a huge area of the northern states and Canada.

As the ice receded 10,000 years ago, gouges in the bedrock filled up with water, creating hundreds of

thousands of clear lakes, many very deep. The bedrock area left behind by the glaciers is called the Laurentian Shield, or more commonly, the Canadian Shield (see map), so these lakes are often called *shield* lakes.

Most shield lakes have changed very little since their creation. A sediment layer has covered some of the deeper portions, but the basins still consist primarily of rock. Because of the low mineral content of the water, most of these lakes are classed as oligotrophic.

On the extreme northern portion of the shield, the climate is so severe that the lakes hold only coldwater

fish, primarily lake trout, grayling and Arctic char. Farther south, many lakes have lake trout in the depths and northern pike in the shallows, but they're not true two-story lakes because the water temperature in the upper story never gets high enough for most warmwater fish.

Many lakes on the southern half of the shield, however, support a variety of warmwater fish in addition to the coldwater species. Throughout most of the northern states and Canadian provinces, walleyes and northern pike are the dominant shallow-water species in these lakes. Some two-story lakes also have smallmouth bass and muskies, but these species don't range as far north. Lake trout predominate in the deep water, although other coldwater species, such as whitefish and burbot, are usually present.

Two-story shield lakes in the northeastern states have a different mix of fish species. Smallmouth bass and chain pickerel dominate the upper story while lake trout and landlocked salmon prevail in the lower. Another type of two-story lake is the deep, steep-sided

ice-block lake (p. 9). Because these lakes have basins of earthen material, or *till*, rather than bedrock, their water is more fertile; most are classed as mesotrophic. Although they don't have a year-round supply of oxygen all the way to the bottom, coldwater fish can find enough cool, oxygenated water in and just below the thermocline during periods when oxygen is too low in the depths.

Because the warmwater and coldwater fish in two-story lakes use separate habitats and consume different foods, there is little competition between them. Smallmouth bass, for instance, seldom go deeper than 30 feet, and lake trout rarely move shallower than 30 feet, except to spawn. Smallmouths feed on crayfish, shiners and other warmwater baitfish, while lake trout eat coldwater baitfish, such as ciscoes and smelt.

The lakes discussed in the two case studies that follow are both shield lakes, but their fish populations differ considerably and so do the methods for fishing them.

Case Study:
Cliff Lake, Ontario

When you're fishing in the shadow of a towering rock wall, it's easy to understand where Cliff Lake got its name.

A classic two-story shield lake with a deep, rocky basin, Cliff Lake has an appealing list of gamefish. You'll find smallmouth bass, walleyes, northern pike and muskies in the warmwater zone, along with yellow perch and shiners for forage. Lake trout swim in the deeper, colder water, where they feed on ciscoes. Good numbers of whitefish occupy the depths.

This surprising assortment of fish results from the variety of habitat. Besides the deep, cold lake trout haunts, the lake's irregular basin has plenty of shallow-water habitat, such as weedy bays for pike and muskies, and rocky reefs and points for smallmouth bass and walleyes.

There are no smelt in Cliff Lake, and their use as bait has recently been banned in northwestern Ontario for fear they will become established and endanger gamefish populations.

Although the surface temperature on Cliff Lake may rise into the 70s in summer, the depths remain frigid, about 43 degrees. Below 70 feet, the temperature changes very little throughout the year. A thermocline generally forms between 25 and 40 feet.

The lake is fed by two small inlets, but most of its water comes from springs. This may explain the higher-than-normal clarity, approximately 15 feet. The clear water can make fishing tough, especially on a calm, clear day.

Even though Cliff Lake is easily accessible by road, fishing pressure is moderate. There are three resorts and one public boat access on the lake, but few private cabins. Most anglers who come to the lake fish for lake trout.

Cliff Lake's reputation for tough fishing probably keeps some anglers away, but those who have taken time to learn the lake enjoy some of the best mixed-bag fishing Canada has to offer.

Other attractions include blueberry picking in August and ruffed grouse hunting in September and October. There's excellent moose hunting, and some hunting for black bear.

Moose are common visitors to the bogs around Cliff Lake

Cliff Lake Physical Data

Acreage	5,739
Average depth	35 ft
Maximum depth	112 ft
Clarity	15 ft
Color	clear
Limits of thermocline	25 to 40 ft
Total phosphorus (parts per billion)	8
Average date of freeze-up	December 1
Average date of ice-out	April 28

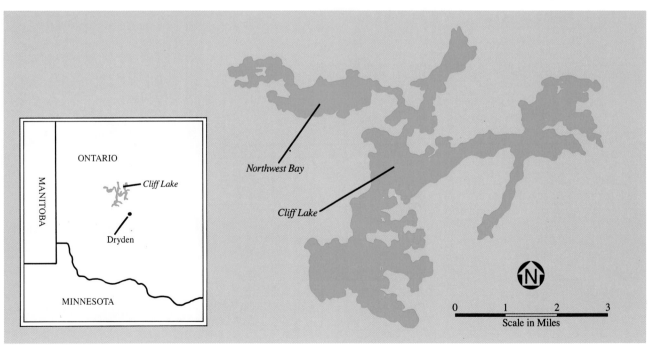

Cliff Lake Habitat (*sample locations of habitats are numbered on aerial photo*)

1. SHALLOW BAYS, 4 feet or less, are good spawning areas for muskies and northerns. On hot summer days, muskies sun themselves in the bays.

2. DEEP BAYS, those with at least 6 feet of water, are prime muskie producers. The best bays have a good growth of cabbage.

3. UNDERWATER EXTENSIONS off points hold smallmouth bass, walleyes and sometimes muskies from late spring through fall.

4. ROCKY REEFS are good spots for walleyes, smallmouths and muskies from late spring through fall. Look for reefs that top off at 10 feet or less.

5. POINTS with a moderate slope draw walleyes, smallmouth bass and a few pike in summer. Walleyes also use these points in spring.

6. STEEP-SLOPING POINTS attract walleyes and smallmouths in fall. The fish change depth more then, and a steeper slope makes it easier to do.

7. ISLANDS that slope gently into deep water are excellent springtime lake trout spots. You'll find the fish at depths of 10 to 40 feet.

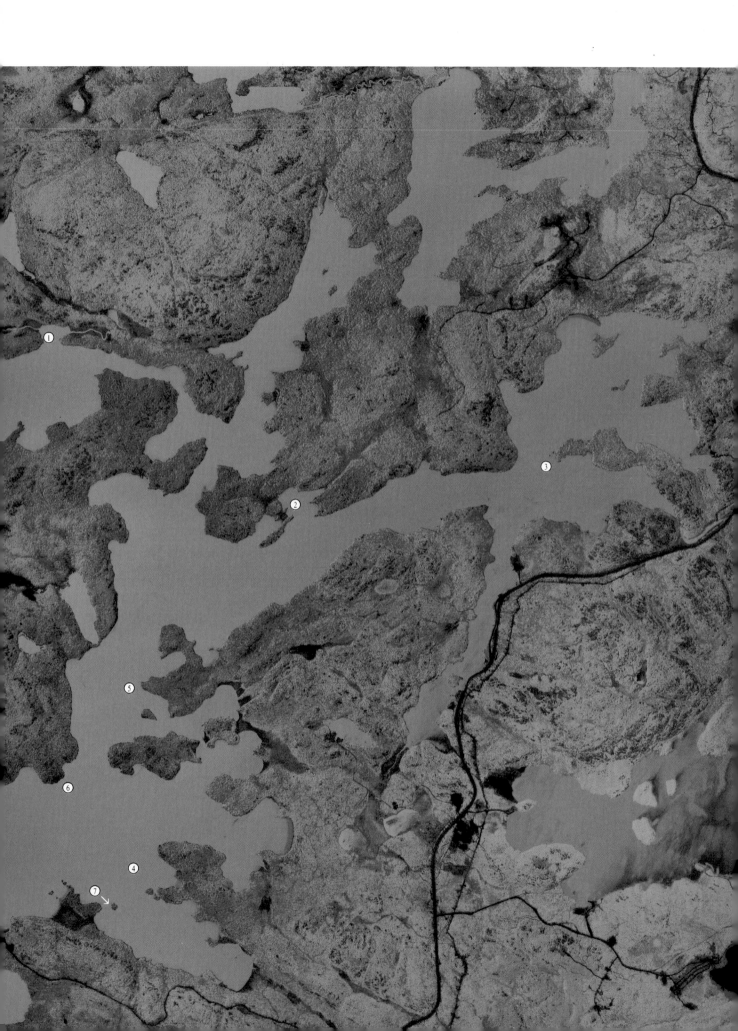

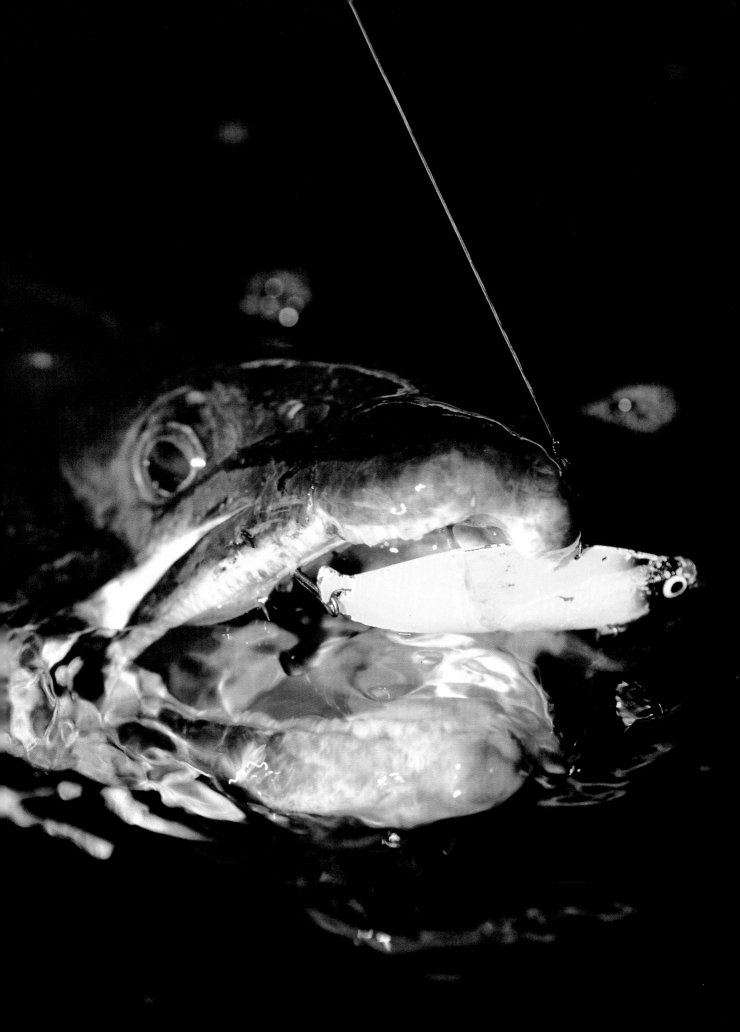

Cliff Lake:
Lake Trout

Lakes you can easily reach by road generally have sub-par lake trout fishing, but Cliff Lake is an exception. Anglers who know where to find them catch plenty of 3- to 5-pounders, and a few over 15. The lake record, taken in the spring of 1990, weighed 29 pounds, 2 ounces.

Shortly after the ice goes out in late April, lakers begin cruising the shallows. You'll find them along most any shoreline, but the prime spots are points and islands with slowly tapering drop-offs. Most of the fish cruise at depths of 10 to 30 feet, but you may find them as deep as 40.

Still-fishing from shore with dead bait, either ciscoes or strips of sucker meat, is a time-proven technique for lakers in spring. But some Cliff Lake anglers have refined the technique by using a multiple-dropper rig (p.62). You can legally use as many as four droppers on a single line, allowing you to fish at different depths so you can find the fish more easily.

You can also catch springtime lakers by casting heavy spoons or jigs tipped with a small piece of sucker meat. Most shore fishermen use a 6-foot, medium-power spinning or baitcasting outfit with 8- to 12-pound mono. These methods work well until about mid-June. When the water temperature exceeds 50°F, the trout begin moving deeper.

In early summer, you'll find them off steep-sloping points and other deep breaks, usually at depths of 40 to 60 feet. But by midsummer, they retreat to holes from 80 to more than 100 feet deep. You can catch them anywhere in the deep holes, although they'll be more concentrated around any deep points and humps in the area.

Trout are easy to locate with a graph because many of them suspend. Often, you'll see some trout close to the bottom and others as much as 30 feet above the bottom.

Once you locate a group of trout, hover over them with a trolling motor and lower a ½-ounce jigging lure or a jig and minnow. If you can hold your position over the fish, you should be able to see your jig descend. Stop it a few feet above the fish, then pull it up with a long sweep of the rod, keeping your line taut as the lure sinks.

Continue to jig the lure above the fish, and set the hook whenever you feel a tap or the jig doesn't sink normally. A 7- to 8-foot medium-power baitcasting outfit with 10-pound mono is ideal for vertical jigging. The long rod gives you a good sweep so you get a strong hookset in the deep water.

When you see trout at various depths, you'll generally have better success if you target the higher fish. The deep ones aren't as active.

It's difficult to keep your line vertical on a windy day, but if you have a heavy anchor and a long rope,

POPULAR LURES for lake trout include: (1) 1-ounce Northland Sting'r Bucktail Jig tipped with a minnow, (2) ½-ounce Heddon Sonar, (3) Acme Kastmaster, (4) Luhr Jensen Diamond King, (5) ½-ounce Northland Airplane Jig tipped with a minnow, (6) Bait-Walker rig tied with a 5-foot leader and a Luhr Jensen Flutter Spoon.

you can anchor in deep water and jig as the boat swings (p. 63).

Another effective technique, especially when the fish are close to the bottom, is wire-lining. Using an extra-stiff rod and a level-wind reel spooled with 20-pound single-strand stainless-steel wire line, lower a three-way-swivel or Bait-Walker rig to the bottom and begin trolling slowly. Let out enough line that you occasionally touch bottom with the sinker. Some anglers maintain that no other method outfishes wire-lining, but many object to the heavy weight on the line because it detracts from the fight.

Downriggers are rapidly becoming popular for trout fishing because they allow you to keep your lure at a precise depth, yet you don't need weight on your line. But downriggers don't work well for bottom-hugging trout; if you run your weights close enough to the bottom to interest the fish, you risk snagging your lures and cannonballs in the rocks.

As the weather cools in September, lakers begin moving toward shallow rocky reefs and points where they'll spawn in early October. During this transition period, you'll find most of the fish at depths of 40 to 80 feet. In years past, anglers wreaked havoc with spawners that were tightly concentrated on the reefs. But the fishing season now closes September 30, so the fish can spawn unmolested.

The season reopens January 1 and by this time, the lake is capped with about 3 feet of ice. The lakers have moved back to the same spots where they spent the summer, although some will be shallower.

Prime wintertime spots are humps that top off at 40 to 60 feet in water at least 30 feet deeper. Most of the fish relate to the top of the reef, but some lie along the dropoff and others suspend over deep water. The best way to catch lakers through the ice is to jig with vibrating blades or with bucktail or airplane jigs tipped with minnows.

Drill a lot of holes, and keep moving until you find the fish. Using a medium-power jigging rod about 3½ feet long and a baitcasting reel spooled with 10-pound mono, start jigging on the bottom and gradually

How to Catch Lake Trout on a Multiple-Dropper Rig

1. TIE a 1½-ounce bell sinker to your 12-pound mono. To make a dropper, tie a size 1 treble hook to one end of a 2-foot piece of 10-pound mono; a snap to the other. Hook on a piece of cut cisco or sucker.

2. LOWER your sinker and one dropper into the desired depth of water, then begin motoring back toward shore. Leave your reel in free-spool so you don't drag the sinker along with you.

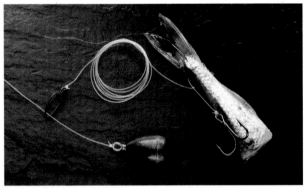

3. ATTACH up to three more droppers at 20- to 30-foot intervals as you motor back toward shore. Just clip the dropper onto your line (inset). The weight of the hook and bait will sink the dropper.

4. PROP UP your rod on a log and make sure your reel is in free-spool. Wrap your line around a pop can. When a trout bites, you'll hear the can rolling. Reel up slack until you feel the weight of the fish, then set the hook.

work the lure upward. As in summer, the "high" fish often bite better than the bottom-huggers.

Tip-up fishing with dead ciscoes also produces a lot of lakers in winter, but jigging allows you to move around more easily. Some anglers set out one tip-up and jig with another line.

Because they inhabit such deep water, lakers show less response to changes in weather than do other gamefish. Open-water anglers prefer fair weather with light winds for easy boat control. Calm weather makes wintertime jigging easier, too.

Lakers will bite any time of day, but you'll seldom catch them after dark. Often, the fastest action is in the middle of the day.

JIGGING works as well for ice fishing as it does in open water. It's much easier to move from hole to hole with a jigging outfit than with a tip-up.

How to Vertical-Jig Using the Swing Technique

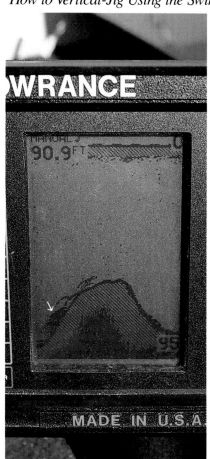  

LOCATE a school of lake trout on a hump or breakline using your graph. Your odds are best if you can find a tight school (arrow).

DROP a heavy anchor attached to a chain and at least 150 feet of rope up-wind of your spot. This way, your anchor will hold in the deep water.

VERTICAL-JIG as the boat swings back and forth on the anchor rope. You'll stay over the fish, yet move enough to cover a good-sized area.

Cliff Lake:

Muskies

Muskies are notorious followers, and those in Cliff Lake are no exception. Some days, you may get more than a dozen follows without a single strike. Other days, they'll grab anything you throw at them.

Cliff Lake has an abundance of medium-sized muskies, fish ranging from 34 to 38 inches. But there are a fair number of fish up to 45 inches and occasionally somebody takes one measuring 50-plus and weighing more than 35 pounds.

The muskies spawn in shallow bays, usually in late May, and remain there for several weeks. But fishing is slow when the season opens on the second Saturday in June; the fish are in poor condition and haven't started to feed heavily.

As the water warms, most muskies move away from the shallow bays into deeper ones. The best summertime bays have a lush growth of cabbage and are within easy reach of water at least 30 feet deep. On warm, clear days, however, muskies often move into the shallower bays to "sun" themselves just below the surface.

Another good summertime muskie hangout is a rocky hump surrounded by deep water. Humps

POPULAR LURES for Cliff Lake muskies include: (1) Cordell Redfin, (2) Blue Fox Super Vibrax Buck, (3) Buchertail Buzzer, (4) Windels Harasser, (5) Suick Thriller, (6) Rapala Magnum.

How to Find Muskies With a "Locator" Lure

CAST a buzzbait or other noisy surface lure in an area where you expect to find muskies. Keep moving and cover a lot of water.

LOOK for boils, follows or any indication that a muskie is around. The fish tend to miss surface lures but still reveal their presence.

CHANGE lures if you see a muskie but it won't strike after another cast or two. Try a bucktail or another lure that runs beneath the surface.

connected to a good-sized feeding flat with a cabbage bed on top usually hold more muskies than small, bald humps.

The muskies really turn on in early August, and the fast action continues through September. You'll still find most of the fish around their summertime spots. But when the water cools in mid-September, some of them move to deeper structure, such as steep points and shoreline breaks. Easy access to deep water is even more important in fall than in summer.

Muskies often turn on when the weather has been hot and muggy for several days. In fall, overcast days are best. You can catch muskies any time of day, but morning fishing tends to be slow.

Bucktails produce the most Cliff Lake muskies, although jerkbaits and minnow plugs are also good choices. Start with relatively small lures in early summer, then switch to larger, deeper-running models as the season progresses.

For casting bucktails and minnow plugs, use a 7-foot medium-heavy baitcasting outfit spooled with 20-pound, low-stretch mono, or 30-pound Dacron. Use a shorter, stiffer rod for jerkbait fishing. Of course, a wire leader is a must.

When the muskies are following but don't want to grab your lure, try something smaller. Or use a buzzbait to locate the fish, then switch to a bucktail (see above).

Cliff Lake:
Walleyes

Walleye anglers on Cliff Lake know the fish can be "here today, gone tomorrow." But if you find them, you can easily catch a limit of 2- to 4-pounders, and there's a shot at one over 10.

Your best odds are in early season, when they're beginning to feed in the shallows after spawning. Look for them on gradually tapering points, on rocky humps near shore, in sand-gravel bays, or in narrows between major lobes of the lake. Usually, they're at depths of 10 feet or less.

When the fish are this shallow, cast to them with a ⅛- to ¼-ounce jig tipped with a minnow. Keep the jig on the bottom and retrieve in short hops. A 6-foot medium-power

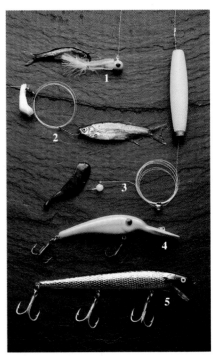

LURES AND RIGS: (1) jig and minnow, (2) slip-sinker rig with size 2 hook and shiner, (3) slip-bobber rig with ⅟₁₆-oz. jig and leech, (4) Shadling, (5) Hellcat.

spinning outfit with 6- to 8-pound mono is ideal for jig fishing. You can also catch walleyes by slow-trolling live-bait rigs baited with minnows, or by casting with crankbaits and minnow plugs. But if the water temperature is below 50 degrees, walleyes may be reluctant to chase a fast-moving lure. And if you troll over them in the shallows with a bait rig, you may spook them.

By early July, walleyes move deeper. They may not go far from the spots where you found them in spring, but they'll be farther down the break, usually at depths of 15 to 30 feet and sometimes as deep as 40. The best spots have a moderate slope.

As in spring, you can catch walleyes on a jig and minnow, or a live-bait rig with a leech or nightcrawler. But when they ignore these offerings, try a slip-bobber rig and a leech. Anchor your boat just off a reef or point where you suspect the fish to be, set the bobber so the bait is about a foot off bottom, and let the leech dangle in front of them. A spinning rod

at least 7 feet long enables you to get a strong hookset when slip-bobber fishing.

When the water starts to cool in fall, walleyes go even deeper. They school more tightly now, usually at depths of 25 to 40 feet. Most fall walleyes are taken with minnows on live-bait rigs.

There's practically no ice fishing for walleyes on Cliff Lake; most anglers concentrate on lake trout.

Because of the clear water, walleye fishing on Cliff Lake is especially tough in calm, sunny weather, but you may catch a few early or late in the day. They bite much better in windy or overcast weather, and feeding periods may extend into midday.

The wind is even more important on Cliff Lake than on lakes with lower clarity. Always look for points or reefs buffeted by the wind. The wave action not only reduces light penetration so the walleyes move shallower, it also blows in plankton, which attracts minnows and spurs walleye feeding activity.

How to Catch Fussy Walleyes on a Slip-Bobber Rig

DROP a marker buoy alongside a school of walleyes. Maybe you caught a few earlier, but they quit biting. Or you simply saw them on your graph.

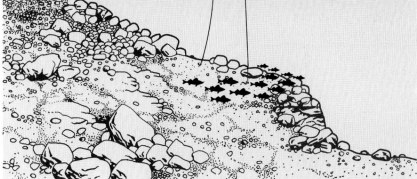

POSITION your boat within casting distance of your marker, then toss out a slip-bobber rig set to the right depth. The fish hold tight to structure, such as an extension from a point; keep your bait in the exact spot. Even negative fish have a hard time ignoring a bait dangled right in their face.

LURES AND RIGS: (1) Floating Rapala, (2) ¼-ounce Northland Fireball Jig and minnow, (3) Gaines Crippled Killer, (4) Rebel Deep Wee R, (5) single-spin spinnerbait, (6) ¼-ounce Gapen Ugly-Bug tipped with a piece of crawler, (7) slip-bobber rig with a size 4 hook and leech.

Cliff Lake:

Smallmouth Bass

With so many big fish such as muskies and lakers in Cliff Lake, smallmouths get little attention. But there are plenty of them, and they provide a lot more action than the "glamour" fish.

In June, when smallmouths concentrate in bays and along shallow, rocky shorelines to spawn, you can catch them by the dozens. They're not big, averaging a little more than a pound, but there's a chance of connecting with a 4- to 6-pounder.

For excitement, try catching them on propbaits. Using a light spinning outfit with 6-pound mono, cast the lure right up to shore and retrieve it with short twitches followed by long pauses. Sometimes the water explodes when a smallmouth takes the lure, but other times, you'll see only a dimple on the surface. Stay alert and set the hook at any hint of a strike.

Another good lure around spawning time is a small floating minnow plug. Cast toward shore and retrieve with sharper, faster twitches so the lure "walks" on the surface.

You can also catch early-season smallmouths on small crankbaits, preferably crayfish or shad patterns, and on ⅛- to ¼-ounce jigs in dark or neutral colors.

Smallmouths are harder to find in summer because they spread out over a wide depth range. Some stay in the shallows; others drop into water more than 25 feet deep. You'll find the largest concentrations on rocky points and on humps that top off at 10 feet or less, but smallmouths will scatter along the entire shoreline. It's not unusual to catch them along with walleyes, although smallmouths tend to be a little shallower.

Jigs and crankbaits produce smallmouths through the summer. When the fish are finicky, tip your jig with either a leech or half a nightcrawler. Or fish the bait on a slip-bobber rig.

You can catch smallmouths well into the fall, but few fishermen go after them. When the fish move out of their summertime spots in mid- to late September, try fishing deep points or humps with a jig and minnow. Don't be afraid to go as deep as 35 feet.

Time of day is not critical, but afternoon fishing is usually best in spring; morning fishing in summer. As in walleye fishing, however, the wind is all-important. If it's buffeting a rocky point or shoreline, you might catch smallmouths in water less than 5 feet deep, even on a hot summer day.

You can catch little smallmouths almost anyplace where the depth is 25 feet or less. But where you find a school of small ones, you probably won't find big ones. Don't waste your time and bait; keep moving until you find an area with fewer but larger fish.

Tips for Finding Smallmouths

LOOK for small rocks, no bigger than a basketball. They hold more crayfish, the smallmouth's favorite food, than do large boulders or slab rock.

WATCH for a mudline or clayline along the bank. Wave action discolors the water and carries in plankton, drawing baitfish and smallmouths.

CHECK any downed trees whose tops are submerged. The branches offer shade, attract baitfish and provide a substrate for insect larvae. Cast into pockets between the branches using a crankbait or spinnerbait.

DETERMINE the right depth using the "high-low" method. While one angler casts a crankbait into shore, the other jigs in deeper water.

TROLL with a deep-diving crankbait along the base of a cliff wall. Smallmouths hold tight to the wall or lie along a projecting lip.

Cliff Lake:
Northern Pike

Northerns are scarce in Cliff Lake, but you may take a few while fishing for muskies. The ones you catch run good sized, however, often over 10 pounds and sometimes as large as 20.

Pike are easiest to catch from ice-out through mid-June. You can find them in shallow bays or around river mouths as they return to the lake after spawning. They go deeper in summer. Some pike move into the same deep bays used by muskies, and others cruise the walleye reefs and points. They return to shallower water in fall.

You can catch pike with the same tackle and lures used for muskies, but spoons and spinnerbaits also work well. Be sure to use a lure that can be retrieved rapidly so you can cover a lot of water.

Northerns bite best on overcast days with a light chop. Fishing during the middle of the day is usually better than in morning or evening.

POPULAR LURES for northern pike in Cliff Lake include: (1) Eppinger Dardevle, (2) Rebel Floating Minnow, (3) Mepps Giant Killer, and (4) Blue Fox Roland Martin Musky Special.

Cliff Lake:
Whitefish

When you're jigging for lakers on Cliff Lake, don't be surprised if you pull up a silvery fish with a small, underslung mouth — a whitefish. These common but overlooked fish are often caught in the same areas and at the same depths as lake trout. And they'll hit the same lures.

You can catch whitefish any time of year, but fishing is best in the first few weeks after ice-out, when they're in water less than 30 feet deep. They also bite well in the winter. Time of day is not important, but they seem to bite better in sunny weather.

Whitefish run big on Cliff Lake, averaging about 3 pounds and topping out at about 8. But for such a large fish, they have a small mouth. So even though they'll take good-sized lures, they prefer something much smaller.

Although whitefish are excellent eating, particularly when smoked, not many anglers fish specifically for them. Those who do commonly use a 1½- to 2-inch jigging spoon tipped with a minnow. Other good lures include small jigs and spinners.

Fly-fishing, while not common on Cliff Lake, is popular in many two-story lakes, especially those with good-sized tributaries. Whitefish congregate around the stream mouths or surface-feed in the open waters of the lake in morning and evening, and you can catch them on dry flies. They often cruise quite rapidly as they feed, so you'll have to watch their movement and "lead" them accordingly.

LURES for whitefish include: (1) Swedish Pimple tipped with a minnow hooked through both lips, (2) Panther Martin spinner, (3) ⅛-ounce marabou jig, (4) ¼-ounce Heddon Sonar.

Case Study:

Sebec Lake, Maine

Sebec Lake and its picture-postcard scenery lure anglers from throughout the East. The nearby mountains provide a gorgeous backdrop and wilderness flavor, despite hundreds of cabins on the lake.

Like Cliff Lake, Sebec is an ice-scour lake (p. 9), formed when a glacier carved a depression in the bedrock. And just as Cliff Lake supports both warmwater and coldwater fish, so does Sebec. But there are some important differences.

Both lakes have smallmouths in the upper story, but instead of northerns, muskies and walleyes, Sebec has chain pickerel and white perch. Both have lake trout in the lower story, but Sebec also has landlocked salmon and a few brook trout. In Cliff, the coldwater forage base is ciscoes; in Sebec, smelt.

Sebec lies within a day's drive of 60 million people, so it's fished much more heavily than Cliff. In addition to the many cabins, or "camps," it has a public boat landing and two fishing resorts.

The lake has two main basins connected by a narrows. The western basin (155 feet deep) supports most of the coldwater fish. The eastern basin (80 feet deep) has mostly warmwater fish, but some lake trout and landlocked salmon are caught in the deeper portions.

Classified as oligotrophic, Sebec has very clear water with only a slight brownish stain. There are about 20 inlets, the largest being Wilson Stream and Ship Pond Stream, and one outlet, the Sebec River.

Lake trout draw the most attention in Sebec, with landlocked salmon a close second. There's a burst of white perch fishing in spring, and interest in smallmouth bass is rapidly increasing.

The open-water fishing season starts at ice-out, which is usually in early May. The season closes September 30. Then it's illegal to fish for *any* species until January 1, after freeze-up.

Ice fishing, mainly for lake trout, has become more popular in recent years and now accounts for about one-third of the total fishing hours on Sebec. The ice-fishing season closes March 31.

The major problem on Sebec, and on many other large lakes in Maine, is overfishing, resulting in decreased fish size. Restrictive size and bag limits have helped, but tighter regulations may be needed.

Another problem: lake trout do not reproduce naturally in the lake. They deposit their eggs on rocky shoals, but for some reason, no young are produced.

Biologists suspected the eggs were left high and dry when the lake dropped in winter, but maintaining higher water levels failed to help.

Some think smelt are the problem. While they're highly touted as a forage fish in Maine, that attitude is not widely shared. True, lake trout thrive on a smelt diet, but in many lakes where smelt have been stocked, lake trout have declined. Although there's no direct proof, many biologists believe smelt prey on the newly hatched trout.

Sebec Lake Physical Data

Acreage	6,803
Average depth	42 ft
Maximum depth	155 ft
Clarity	25 ft
Color	clear to slight coffee stain
Total phosphorus (parts per billion)	3
Limits of thermocline	20 to 30 ft
Average date of freeze-up	mid-December
Average date of ice-out	early May

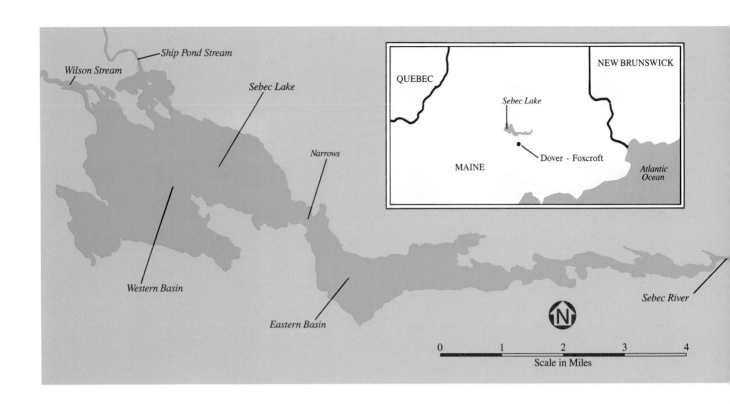

Ship Pond Stream

Wilson Stream

Sebec Lake

Narrows

Western Basin

Eastern Basin

Sebec River

QUEBEC

NEW BRUNSWICK

Sebec Lake

Dover - Foxcroft

MAINE

Atlantic Ocean

N

0   1   2   3   4
Scale in Miles

Sebec Lake Habitat (*sample locations of habitats are numbered on NASA photo*)

1. DEEP POOLS on inlets collect landlocks. They follow smelt into the streams in spring; they move in to spawn in fall. Some pools also hold smallmouths.

2. SAND FLATS, especially those around the mouth of Wilson Stream, attract lake trout and landlocked salmon in spring and fall.

5. WEEDY, SOFT-BOTTOMED COVES make excellent year-round habitat for pickerel. They also attract white perch in spring and smallmouth bass in summer.

6. SHELVES with scattered boulders extend hundreds of feet into the lake along some shorelines. Smallmouths use the shelves from spring through fall.

NASA High Altitude Photograph

3. EXTENDED LIPS off major points hold lake trout and landlocked salmon in summer and fall. The fish often concentrate along the base of the drop-off.

4. ROCKY POINTS are prime locations for smallmouths from early summer through fall. Look for slowly tapering points with plenty of boulders.

7. ROCKY HUMPS that top off at 10 feet or less hold some smallmouths in summer and fall, although they don't produce as consistently as shoreline structure.

8. THE NARROWS between the two major basins is a good spot for lake trout and landlocked salmon in summer and fall. Look for the deepest holes in the narrows.

Sebec Lake:

Lake Trout

Sebec's icy depths and huge smelt crop make it one of Maine's premier lake trout lakes. Despite the heavy fishing pressure, the lake produces some big trout, including a 25-pounder, caught by an ice fisherman in 1989. Most of the fish run 3 to 5 pounds; the minimum legal size is 18 inches (about 2 pounds).

Practically everyone in Maine and southeastern Canada refers to lake trout by their French-Canadian name, *togue*. The fish are not native to Sebec and were first stocked in the early 1960s. Since they do not reproduce naturally in the lake, populations must be maintained by stocking. The deep western basin and the narrows have the best togue fishing; most of the eastern basin is too shallow and warm.

Shortly after ice-out, usually in early May, smelt begin moving into Wilson Stream to spawn. Large schools cruise the sand flats near the stream mouth, with the togue in close pursuit. The traditional method for catching togue throughout the open-water season is lead-line trolling. You'll need a 7- to 8-foot medium-power trolling rod and a high-speed trolling reel capable of holding 150 yards of lead-core line, 18- to 40-pound-test. The line should be color-coded at 10-yard intervals.

You can use a variety of baits and lures for lead-lining, but most veteran Sebec anglers believe that a smelt, preferably a live one, will outfish anything else. Suckers, golden shiners, small spoons and minnow plugs also catch a lot of fish.

Start trolling in the vicinity of the stream mouth, letting out enough line to get down 10 to 25 feet. To reach the right depth, "count the colors." As a rule, one 10-yard section or color gets you down about 5 feet. If you're fishing with a friend, it pays to try different color counts (opposite page). Keep experimenting until one of you finds the right depth.

Anglers on Sebec and many other Maine lakes often attach large attractors, such as cowbells, ahead of

their lure or bait. Another popular attractor is a Murray Flasher, an oversized copper spinner blade about 6 inches long. The big blade not only attracts togue, it serves as a speed and bottom indicator, transmitting its strong beat up the line and through the rod. Any change in the tempo of the beat signals a change in trolling speed. If the beat stops, the blade has hit bottom, so you must reel in some line. Try to keep the rig near bottom, but don't let it drag.

You can also catch togue in spring by still-fishing or slowly drifting around the stream mouth with a smelt, sucker or shiner on a slip-sinker rig. Use a medium-power spinning outfit with 6- to 10-pound mono.

By late May, smelt have completed spawning and moved back into the lake. They school up along steep shoreline breaks, off the ends of major points, on deep mud flats and in the narrows. Look for togue in the same areas, at depths of 35 to 55 feet in early summer; 60 to 80 feet in late summer. The fish are usually close to the bottom, but they may suspend as much as 20 feet off bottom on sunny days. The baits, lures and attractors used in spring work equally well in summer.

When the togue go deep, it's difficult to troll with lead-core line. You'll wear yourself out reeling in 15 or more colors, and if you're trolling with two or more lines, they may cross when you make a turn or a crosswind blows you off course.

Trolling with wire line solves the problem. You'll need a stiff rod with a roller tip and a level-wind trolling reel spooled with at least 100 yards of single-strand stainless steel wire, about 20-pound test. Attach the wire to a three-way swivel, then add a 15-pound mono dropper with an 8-ounce weight and a 6-foot leader of 10-pound mono. Some anglers don't like the idea of trolling with this much weight, but you'll need only about a fourth as much line to reach bottom.

LURES AND RIGS include: (1) three-way swivel rig with 8-ounce weight and Sutton spoon, (2) slip-sinker rig with size 2 hook and shiner, (3) Mooselook Wobbler, (4) Murray Flasher with a tandem-hook rig, (5) Bomber Long A. For ice fishing, use a (6) French Hooker lead fish or (7) split-shot rig with size 2 hook and shiner on a tip-up.

How to Troll With Lead-core Line

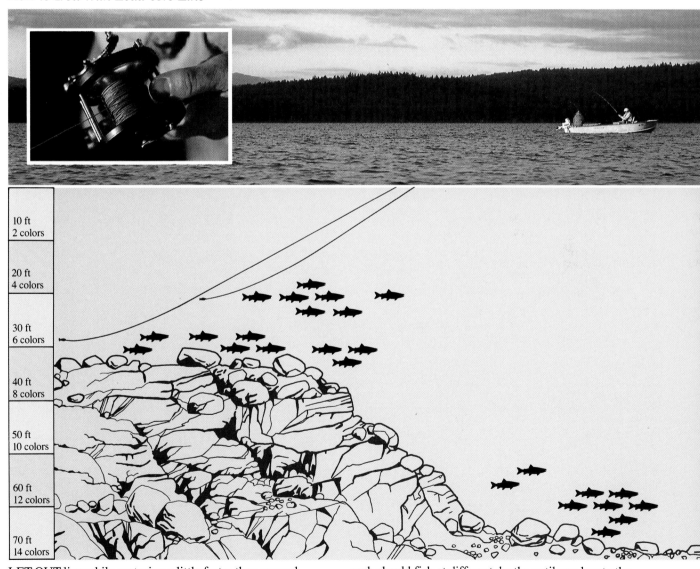

10 ft
2 colors

20 ft
4 colors

30 ft
6 colors

40 ft
8 colors

50 ft
10 colors

60 ft
12 colors

70 ft
14 colors

LET OUT line while motoring a little faster than normal trolling speed. Remember to count the colors (inset) as the line pays out, then reduce your speed. With two anglers, each should fish at different depths until you locate the fish. The scale along the left margin gives you an idea of how deep your lures will run.

Some anglers use downriggers, but they don't work well when togue are close to the bottom.

The summer pattern continues into fall, although some of the fish move back to the sandy flats around the stream mouth. They gradually move shallower as the water cools, and by mid-September, they're in depths of 20 to 45 feet.

According to creel surveys, ice fishermen on Sebec catch togue at about three times the rate of open-water fishermen. Togue are found in the same areas as in summer, but at depths of 30 to 50 feet. Anglers focus on any spots that have large rocks or break sharply into deep water.

Tip-ups, or "traps" as they're often called in the Northeast, account for most of the togue taken through the ice. All you have to do is bait up with a live smelt, sucker or shiner, lower the rig to bottom, set the flag and wait for it to trip.

Another effective method is jigging with a Swedish Pimple or a heavy jigging lure called a lead fish. You can fish them plain or tip them with a 1- to 2-inch piece of cut smelt or sucker.

Togue seem to bite best in overcast weather with little wind. Your odds are better in morning and evening than in midday, although ice fishermen often catch togue all day long.

Tip-ups produce some good-sized togue in Sebec

HOOK a smelt on a size 6 tandem-hook setup with the front hook rigged to slip. Insert the treble about two-thirds of the way back, then slide the single hook up the line and hook the smelt through the lips (inset).

AVOID rigging the smelt with a bend in the body. A bend makes it spin, rather than track naturally.

SELECT male smelt (top) instead of females (bottom). Smelt are usually collected in spring, then frozen, so the females are full of eggs. They have soft bellies that tend to rip open as you troll.

LOCATE togue by watching for plumes of smelt (arrow) on your graph. Often the togue lie just beneath the smelt.

INSTALL a roller tip on your lead-lining rod to reduce line wear. Without a roller tip, the expensive line tends to fray, so you'll have to replace it more often.

DRAG a 5-gallon bucket tied to a harness if your motor trolls too fast. A bucket makes it possible to troll with even the largest motors.

Landlocks jumping the falls on Wilson Stream

Sebec Lake:

Landlocked Salmon

Landlocked salmon, the smaller cousin of the sea-going Atlantic salmon, spend their entire life in fresh water. Atlantics spawn in large streams along the North Atlantic coast, and the young salmon spend the first two years of life there. But the glaciers isolated some populations, preventing the fish from reaching the sea.

Today, "landlocks" still spawn in streams, but instead of returning to the sea, they return to inland lakes such as Sebec.

Many regard Atlantic salmon as the foremost sportfish in the world, mainly because of their leaping ability. Landlocks, though considerably smaller, possess the same leaping skills. When you hook one, its first instinct is to rocket from the water, shaking its head violently to throw the hook.

Like togue, landlocks are coldwater fish, but they don't require water quite as frigid. The togue's ideal temperature range is 48 to 52° F; the landlock's, 53 to 59.

As soon as the ice goes out, usually early May, landlocks move into Wilson Stream to feed on smelt, which are working their way upstream to spawn. You can catch some salmon in the stream itself, as far upstream as the falls. But most of the fish are caught on sand flats around the stream mouth. The minimum legal size is 14 inches.

Prior to spawning, smelt roam the sand flats, usually in depths of 10 to 20 feet. Both landlocks and togue follow the smelt schools, but the salmon swim higher in the water. You'll seldom find them deeper than 10 feet, and sometimes they're right on the surface.

When the fish are this shallow, you can catch them by trolling a small spoon, streamer fly or smelt on a light spinning outfit with 6-pound mono. Or troll with a 5- or 6-weight fly rod with a sink-tip line.

Some anglers troll with lead-core line, but most of the fish weigh less than 2 pounds, and the heavy line detracts from the fight.

LURES AND RIGS for landlocked salmon include: (1) Gray Ghost streamer, (2) Mooselook Wobbler, (3) split-shot rig with size 2 hook and shiner, which can also be used on a tip-up for ice fishing.

Another simple but effective method is still-fishing or drifting around the stream mouth with a smelt or shiner on a split-shot rig.

By early June, most smelt have pulled away from the stream mouth, and so have the salmon. Because the salmon and the togue are both following the smelt schools, you'll find them in the same areas: along steep shoreline breaks, off the ends of major points, on deep mud flats and in the narrows. But the salmon usually run a little shallower than the togue. Look for them in 30 to 60 feet of water, suspended 10 to 20 feet off bottom.

Lead-lining with spoons, streamers or smelt is the traditional summertime method for landlocks, but more and more anglers are switching to downriggers and lighter tackle. With a light, 7- to 8-foot spinning or baitcasting outfit and 8-pound mono, even a 16-inch salmon can give you a good tussle.

You'll find some salmon in their summer locations until mid-September, but by then, many have moved into Wilson Stream and Ship Pond Stream, where they'll spawn in October. You can catch some salmon in pools in the streams, but most are taken around

Tips for Catching Landlocks

USE a mini-downrigger instead of lead-core line for landlocks. The tiny downrigger, which attaches easily to the gunwale of a small boat, gives you better depth control, and there's no heavy line to inhibit the fight.

WORK the pools on spawning streams to catch landlocks in fall. Most anglers use worms, either below a bobber or on a split-shot rig. Or fan-cast the pool with a small spinner tipped with a piece of worm.

Tip-ups work well for landlocks

the mouth of Wilson Stream. Use the same techniques as in summer, but work depths from the surface down to 25 feet. The season closes September 30.

Ice fishing for landlocks on Sebec can be tough. Tip-up fishermen using live smelt, shiners or worms take a few salmon around the mouth of Wilson Stream, but most ice fisherman go after togue.

The prime time to catch landlocked salmon is early morning, from sunrise to about 11 a.m. There's another flurry in the evening, but it doesn't last as long. Generally, landlocks bite best on sunny days with little or no wind.

Sebec Lake:
Smallmouth Bass

In Maine, practically all fish management efforts are directed toward coldwater fish. The policy for smallmouths and other warm-water fish is "containment": keep them from spreading to other waters. In some coldwater lakes, including Sebec, there is still no bag limit on smallmouths, and it's legal to take them during the spawning season.

Many anglers, however, are trying to change their state's management philosophy. They recognize the smallmouth's value as a sportfish and feel the state should update its smallmouth program.

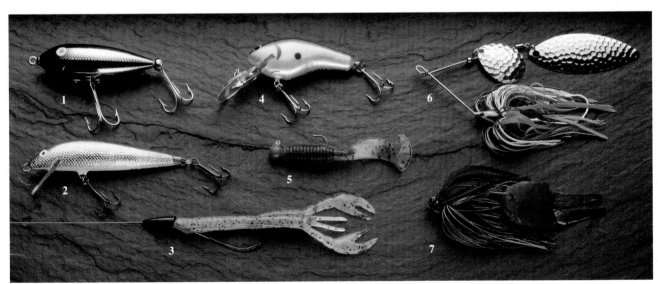

LURES include: (1) Heddon Baby Zara, (2) A.C. Shiner 375, (3) 4-inch crawworm Texas rigged on a 1/0 hook, (4) Bagley Killer B-II Dredge, (5) 1/8-ounce curly-tail jig, (6) Northland Reed Runner, (7) 1/4-ounce jig and pork frog.

Not that smallmouths in Sebec are doing poorly on their own. Despite the lack of regulation, the lake has an impressive smallmouth population. Most run 1 to 2 pounds, and there are plenty of 2 to 4-pounders. The minimum legal size is 12 inches.

In mid-May, smallmouths begin moving into shallow coves and onto shoreline flats where they'll spawn. The males build nests, usually on the deep side of a boulder, in water 2 to 10 feet deep. The females join them in late May, and spawning begins. Most spawning is completed by mid-June, although males guard the nest for another week or two.

To catch smallmouths around spawning time, move slowly over a shallow, rocky, shoreline flat with a quiet electric trolling motor. Using a medium-power spinning outfit or a light baitcasting outfit with 6- to 8-pound mono, cast to any large boulders. Be sure to wear polarized sunglasses so you can spot the fish on their nests.

Smallmouths instinctively attack anything that comes too close to their nest, so almost any kind of lure will work. Try twitching a 4-inch minnow plug or steadily retrieving a ¼-ounce spinnerbait over the nest. Another technique that practically always works: cast a ⅛-to ¼-ounce jig just past the nest and retrieve it so it falls into the nest. Then just leave it. A bass may tolerate it for awhile, but will eventually pick it up. When fishing this way, use a light-colored jig. This way, you'll see it disappear when a fish grabs it, so you'll know when to set the hook. Live bait is illegal until June 21.

Springtime fishing is best in calm, sunny weather, after the water reaches 60° F. These conditions make it easier to spot likely cover and nesting smallmouths. You can catch fish all day, but they bite best in late afternoon.

Shoreline flats, especially the ones that extend well into the lake and drop rapidly into deep water, continue to produce through the summer. Some of the better flats have scattered cabbage beds.

Most of the flats don't have much cover, so smallmouths relate to some type of object or anything that's different. If there are no weeds, look for rocks, stick-ups or slight depressions. On sunny days, look for the fish in deeper water just off the edge of the flat.

You'll also find summertime smallmouths around long points, docks and rocky humps that top off at 10 feet or less. Fish a little deeper than you would in spring, usually 5 to 12 feet.

The lures used in spring will also work in summer. Other good choices, especially in deeper water or weedy cover, include a Texas-rigged plastic worm or crayfish imitation, a jig-and-pig and a stickbait. In Sebec's clear water, dark or natural colors seem to work best. Smallmouths will swim up as much as 20 feet to take a stickbait walked across the surface.

In summer, smallmouths bite best in cloudy weather with a light, onshore breeze. On calm, sunny days, the fish move to the edges of the breaks; they may go as deep as 25 feet. They're most active in morning and evening.

The pattern changes very little in early fall. Smallmouths go deep in late fall, but the fishing season closes at the end of September.

Tips for Finding Smallmouths

ROCKY NARROWS leading into bays are ideal smallmouth spots. The large rocks provide cover, and the wind-generated current draws baitfish.

SCATTERED BOULDERS on shoreline shelves hold smallmouths from spring through fall. Work the shady side of the boulders.

SPAWNING BEDS are usually built alongside a boulder. The fish fan away the silt, and the beds appear as clean spots on the bottom.

Sebec Lake:
Chain Pickerel

There's no shortage of pickerel in Sebec's weedy coves. All you have to do is toss your lure into a patch of sedge or cabbage and you'll probably catch one. Top lure choices include spinnerbaits, stickbaits, rubber frogs and minnow plugs.

Another good technique is working a live shiner or frog through or alongside the weeds. Using light spinning tackle, 6- to 8-pound mono and a thin wire leader, hook the bait through the lips, then cast it into the weeds. Let it swim over the weedtops and into any pockets. Fish the bait unweighted, or add a small split-shot.

Pickerel spend the entire year in the weedy, soft-bottomed coves, usually at depths of 2 to 10 feet, although they sometimes go as deep as 15. They're willing biters, ready to take a bait in any weather and at any time of day.

Compared to most area lakes, Sebec has good-sized pickerel. They average about 1½ pounds, and there's a chance of catching one from 4 to 6.

LURES AND RIGS include: (1) Griffin Ol' Line Sides, (2) Lindy Spinnerbait, (3) Super Frog, (4) Cordell Red Fin, (5) live-bait rig tied with Sevenstrand wire and a size 2 hook and baited with a shiner.

Sebec Lake:
White Perch

When the white perch are running on Sebec, anglers flock to the lake to get in on the fast action. You can catch fish by the dozens, and they run big, averaging about ¾ pound and topping out at 2½.

Beginning in late May, when the water temperature reaches the mid-50s, schools of white perch move into shallow, weedy bays and inlet streams to spawn. Using a light spinning outfit with 6-pound mono, cast a spinner tipped with a worm into the shallows and retrieve slowly. Or just use a plain worm on a split-shot rig, with or without a float. Small jigs and minnow plugs will also work.

White perch bite best in warm weather. You can catch them all day long, but they're especially vulnerable at night. Bright lights seem to attract them, so after dark, anglers set up lanterns in the weedy bays.

By mid-June, spawning is completed and the fish scatter to the main lake. They're hard to find the rest of the year, but salmon trollers catch a few by accident.

LURES AND RIGS for white perch include: (1) bobber rig tied with a size 4 hook and baited with a worm, (2) ¹⁄₁₆-ounce Garland Mini Jig, (3) Blue Fox Vibrax spinner with a piece of worm, (4) Bagley Bang-O-Lure.

Midwestern Walleye Lakes

*These big, windswept lakes offer
a potpourri of gamefish,
but the walleye is king*

Practically any type of lake can hold walleyes. They're found in shallow weed-choked lakes dominated by rough fish, deep, clear lake trout lakes, and everything in between.

But the sandy, windswept, moderately fertile lakes found throughout the Midwest support the best walleye populations. Most are ice-block lakes or lakes formed in depressions on the glacial moraine (p. 8), so they have basins of glacial till consisting mainly of sand and gravel and sometimes boulders.

These lakes generally have a healthy crop of yellow perch, the walleye's favorite food. Wave action exposes rubble along the shoreline, creating ideal spawning habitat. The constant water movement prevents the eggs from silting over and keeps them aerated.

Besides walleyes and yellow perch, a wide variety of other gamefish inhabit lakes of this type. Almost all have northern pike, largemouth bass, sunfish and crappies. Some also produce smallmouth bass and a few have muskies.

Although walleyes are found in some very small lakes, they're better suited to big lakes. Most small lakes lack sufficient wave action for successful spawning, so walleyes must be stocked. For the same reason, roundish lakes are better than long, narrow ones. No matter which way the wind blows during the spawning season, there will always be a wind-swept shoreline where walleyes can spawn successfully.

Many anglers have the idea that a good walleye lake must be deep and clear, but that is not necessarily the case. In fact, many of the best walleye lakes are shallow with moderate to low clarity. Minnesota's Mille Lacs Lake, for instance, averages only 21 feet

deep with a maximum depth of 43 feet. The clarity, as determined by a Secchi disc, is about 7 feet. Wisconsin's Lake Winnebago averages 15 feet deep with a maximum depth of 21 feet and a clarity of 3 feet.

Walleyes spend most of their time in water less than 30 feet deep, although they occasionally go deeper to find food. Practically all of a shallow lake is walleye

habitat, but in a deep lake, walleyes are found only along the shorelines and on shallow midlake bars. Consequently, a shallow lake can support several times more walleyes than a deep one.

Because of the walleye's popularity throughout the Midwest, many well-known lakes are heavily fished. The average walleye size has declined and trophies have become less frequent. To combat the problem, some natural resources agencies are imposing restrictions to limit the catch of large walleyes.

Anglers interested in catching a trophy would be well advised to bypass the heavily fished lakes and concentrate on lesser-known lakes with fewer but bigger walleyes.

Case Study:

Woman Lake, Minnesota

Versatility pays when fishing Woman Lake. Though most anglers concentrate on walleyes, there's a good chance of catching largemouth and smallmouth bass, northern pike, crappies, bluegills and jumbo perch, not to speak of trophy-caliber muskies.

Classified as mesotrophic, Woman Lake shares the qualities of many other first-rate midwestern walleye lakes. It has a broad, shallow basin and a bottom

consisting mostly of sand and rubble. The water clarity, however, is much greater than that of a typical walleye lake, measuring 10 to 14 feet most of the year.

Like many other shallow, windswept walleye lakes, Woman Lake does not stratify into distinct temperature layers. During the hottest part of the summer, the surface is only a few degrees warmer than the bottom.

Fed mainly by the Boy River, Woman Lake's water level remains quite stable. Long-term fluctuations are seldom more than a foot from the normal level. The lake drains into a series of other small lakes, into Leech Lake, and then into the Mississippi River.

Woman Lake was formed when a huge ice block buried in the glacial moraine slowly melted (p. 9). Like the hilly terrain surrounding the lake, the bottom is a maze of structure. Spanning the center of the lake is a huge sand-gravel flat with many points and inside turns along its perimeter. Dozens of gravel and rock bars dot the western half of the lake. There are several holes at least 40 feet deep, with the deepest measuring 60 feet.

MINNESOTA
ONTARIO
NORTH DAKOTA
Lake Superior
Leech Lake
Mississippi River
Woman Lake
Longville
WISCONSIN

Girl Lake
Broadwater Bay
Woman Lake
Boy River
Child Lake
Boy River
Horseshoe Island

N

0   1   2
Scale in Miles

Joining the main lake are several large bays, two of which in turn connect to smaller lakes, Girl Lake and Child Lake. The bays and smaller lakes differ greatly from the main lake. They have a softer bottom and considerably more vegetation.

The wide variety of fish species in Woman Lake is a direct result of the diverse habitat. The main body of the lake is best suited to walleyes, perch, smallmouth bass, northern pike and muskies. The bays and smaller lakes are better for largemouth bass, bluegills and crappies.

As in most good walleye lakes, perch are the primary forage fish. But Woman Lake also supports healthy populations of ciscoes, shiners, bullheads and small panfish, all potential foods for walleyes and other predator fish.

Private cabins and homes ring Woman Lake's shoreline, and 12 fishing resorts offer cabins, boats, motors and bait. There are two public access sites on Woman Lake itself. Access is also possible through Girl Lake. Despite the development and heavy use, pollution is not a problem. Because of its large size

(over 3 miles across), rounded shape and expanses of shallow water, Woman Lake gets rough on windy days. Most anglers use deep, 16- to 18-foot semi-V aluminum boats powered by 25- to 50-hp motors. A depth finder is a must for finding the bars and following the irregular breaklines.

Although most of the fishing on Woman Lake takes place from mid-May through August, there is quite a bit of fall fishing. Ice anglers concentrate mainly on walleyes, perch and crappies.

Woman Lake Physical Data

Acreage	4,782
Average depth	25 ft
Maximum depth	60 ft
Clarity	4 to 12 ft
Color	light green
Total phosphorus (parts per billion)	20
Thermocline	none
Average date of freeze-up	November 25
Average date of ice-out	April 24

Woman Lake Habitat (sample locations of habitats are numbered on NASA photo)

1. DOCKS, especially those near the inside weedline, draw largemouths and bluegills in summer and fall. Look for the fish on the shady side.

2. OLD BULRUSHES hold spawning crappies, bluegills and largemouth bass. Some bass stay in the rushes until early to mid-fall.

3. SLOP provides heavy shade, so it makes excellent bass cover from late spring through fall. It consists of lily pads, wild rice and submerged weeds.

4. RICE BEDS offer overhead cover for largemouths and bluegills. The rice lies flat on the water in early summer; later, it stands upright.

5. CABBAGE BEDS on midlake humps attract muskies, northerns and walleyes in summer. The best cabbage humps have deep water nearby.

6. EXTENDED LIPS off main-lake points are good walleye spots. You'll find the fish along the drop-off during the day and on the lip at night.

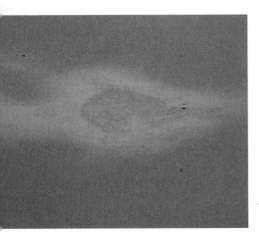

7. LARGE MIDLAKE FLATS hold walleyes, muskies and northern pike in summer and fall. Look for weedbeds, sharp points or dips in the breakline.

8. ROCKY REEFS that top off at 8 feet or less hold walleyes and smallmouths early in the season; smallmouths use the reefs through the summer.

9. BOAT CANALS in shallow bays provide access for property owners. Bluegills and largemouth bass spawn in the openings.

Woman Lake:
Walleyes

Timing is the key to catching walleyes on Woman Lake. Because of its clarity, fishing is tough on calm, sunny days. Most walleyes are caught in cloudy, breezy weather or at night.

In a lake this clear, cover is extremely important to walleyes. To avoid bright light, they spend most of their time near weeds or in the shade of boulders.

Cover is least important in spring because of the low angle of the sun. After the season opens in mid-May, walleyes cruise the shallows in search of food. Look for them on points and inside turns along sandy shoreline breaks, and on rocky midlake humps. Exactly where they'll be depends mainly on wind. A breakline or hump buffeted by the wind will hold more walleyes than a sheltered one. Another attraction is sandgrass on the bottom.

Night fishing with a slip-bobber and leech accounts for a good share of the walleyes in spring. About half an hour before sunset, anchor on the edge of a break and

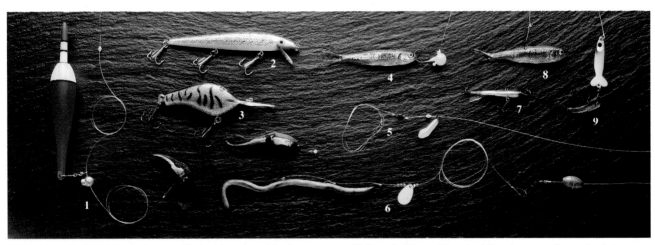

LURES AND RIGS include: (1) slip-bobber rig with size 4 hook and leech, (2) Rebel Minnow Floater, (3) Poe's Series 300 crankbait, (4) ¼-ounce Fireball Jig and shiner, (5) Roach Rig and leech, (6) spinner and crawler harness. For ice fishing: (7) W-5 Jigging Rapala, (8) shiner rig for tip-ups, (9) Fire-Eye Minnow and minnow tail.

cast into 4 to 8 feet of water. Or try trolling with a shallow-running minnow plug. The fish usually bite for three or four hours after dark.

During the day, most walleyes hang along the edge of the break at depths of 12 to 18 feet. You can catch them by slow-trolling a slip-sinker rig baited with a leech or by casting with a jig and minnow.

How well the fish bite depends on how much time has elapsed after spawning. Normally, walleyes finish spawning by late April and are biting by the opener. But in a late spring, spawning extends well into May. The season opens before the females have recuperated, so anglers catch only the males, which run considerably smaller.

By mid-June, submerged weeds, particularly cabbage, become a key element. You'll find walleyes near cabbage beds along shoreline breaks, on extended points and on midlake bars and flats. On cloudy or windy days, they feed along the edge of the weeds; in bright sun, they duck into the weeds. Because the weeds offer shade, walleyes can stay at depths of 12 to 18 feet through the summer. An ordinary slip-sinker rig baited with a leech or crawler is a good choice for summertime walleyes, but some anglers prefer spinner-live bait rigs.

Another popular summertime technique is trolling at night with good-sized minnow plugs or crankbaits. Troll in 8 to 10 feet of water along the tops of the midlake flats, but stay near the drop-off.

By mid-September, most walleyes go deeper, but at night they move back into the weeds, especially green ones. During the day, you'll find them on the same structure as in summer, but at depths of 25 to 35 feet. They're easy to find with a good graph. Hard-bottomed

structure that slopes rapidly usually holds more walleyes than structure that tapers gradually. Once the walleyes go deep, midday fishing improves. The fish are feeding more actively, so they prefer bigger baits. Try a 3- to 4-inch minnow, such as a shiner or redtail chub, on a jig or slip-sinker rig.

As soon as the ice is safe, look for walleyes at depths of 10 to 12 feet on points along the midlake flats. After mid-January, you're more likely to find them at 18 to 30 feet, on the same points or on the ends of cabbage humps. But they may be deeper in early season and shallower in late season, depending on light penetration.

Early or late in the day, in cloudy weather, or under heavy snow cover, they're apt to be shallow; in midday, in sunny weather, or under light snow cover, they usually go deep.

To locate walleyes, try setting a tip-up baited with a shiner along the base of the drop-off, then jig with a second line in the shallower water.

Whether you're jigging or fishing with tip-ups, it's important to use light tackle. For tip-up fishing, use a 6-pound mono leader, a split-shot or two and a size 4 hook; for jigging, a 3-foot, medium-power jigging rod, a small spinning reel and 6-pound mono.

Tip-ups help find walleyes quickly

Tips for Finding Walleyes

LOCATE schools of walleyes by zigzagging along a breakline while watching your depth finder. A video or liquid crystal with a fast sweep speed works best for high-speed sounding.

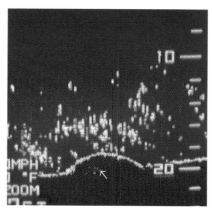

WATCH for "blips" just off bottom or bumps on the bottom. If you see a little "air" between the bump and the bottom (arrow), it's probably a bottom-hugging walleye.

LINE UP two distant objects to get an exact bearing on a midlake walleye reef. Then motor along that line, sounding with your depth finder to locate the precise spot.

Woman Lake:

Muskies

In muskie-fishing circles, Woman Lake is considered a tough lake to master. Its muskie population is much lower than in other nearby lakes, but each year it produces some trophy-class fish. In 1987, for instance, Woman Lake yielded Minnesota's biggest muskie of the year — a 52-incher weighing 40 pounds, 3 ounces.

To have a reasonable chance of connecting with a muskie, you must carefully select your fishing times and locations. The season opens in mid-June, about three weeks after the muskies complete spawning, but fishing is slow until mid-July. By this time, most muskies have moved away from shoreline structure and are concentrating around offshore bars and humps, especially those with a mixture of rocks and cabbage on the bottom.

The best muskie bars and humps top off at 10 feet or less, but are near water at least 30 feet deep. The cabbage is relatively thick and has a distinct edge where the structure breaks into deeper water.

Clean rock bars and weedy flats also produce a few muskies, but your odds are much better if you work the cabbage bars and humps.

The muskies feed most heavily in hot, muggy, stable weather, particularly if there's a southerly breeze and light cloud cover. You'll see the fastest action early and late in the

With a cradle, you can land and release muskies without injuring them

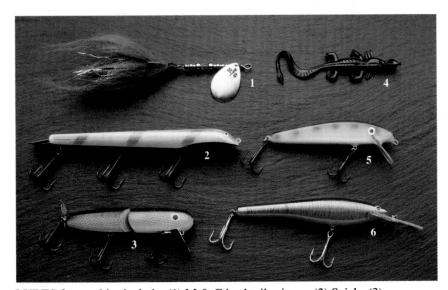

LURES for muskies include: (1) M & G bucktail spinner, (2) Suick, (3) Mouldy's Hawg Wobbler, (4) ⅜-ounce jig with lizard tail, (5) Cobb's Minnow Bait, (6) Bagley DB-08.

day, with some activity at night. During favorable weather and peak feeding periods, muskies will hold on shallower portions of the structure, usually at depths of 4 to 8 feet. Otherwise, they'll be deeper, from 8 to 20 feet.

Most muskie addicts carry two rods: a 6½- to 7-foot bucktail rod with a stiff butt and light tip, and a 5½- to 6-foot "pool cue" for jerkbaits.

The latter must be stiff enough to break a muskie's grip on a wooden plug so you can sink the hooks. Both outfits should be rigged with 30- to 40-pound Dacron line and a heavy steel leader (preferably solid wire).

Woman Lake muskies have a variety of good-sized baitfish to choose from. Suckers and ciscoes from 13 to 18 inches make up a sizable part of their diet, so it pays to use big lures.

Bucktails work best when you're scouting for muskies because you can retrieve them rapidly and cover a lot of water quickly. Most experts prefer dark colors on dark days; bright on bright days. A heavy-duty level-wind baitcasting reel with a high gear ratio allows you to reel fast without tiring your arm.

When a muskie follows your bucktail but won't hit, try casting a jerkbait. The erratic darting action often makes the difference.

If you spot a muskie, but it won't strike, don't continue to pester it with a hodge-podge of different lures. It's better to leave the fish alone for a few hours, then come back to the exact spot two or three hours later for a few more casts. If that doesn't work, wait a few hours more, then try again. Chances are, the fish will stay in the area where you last saw it, and you'll eventually find it in the right mood.

Muskies hang around these weedy offshore bars and humps into late fall, although they start roaming more when the weeds begin to die off in early September. If you can find green weeds, they'll often hold fish, but so will clean rocky humps, points and inside turns along breaklines.

In October, the fish move to steeper breaks and begin to congregate in small groups. The big fish feed heavily in preparation for winter, so this is the best time to catch a trophy. The fastest late-fall action comes late in the afternoon in overcast weather.

As a rule, the fish hold tighter to the bottom this time of year, so you may have to switch to deeper-running lures, such as large crankbaits and jigs. A big sucker fished beneath a bobber also works well.

Muskies continue to bite through October and into November, but the action slows considerably once the water temperature drops below 40° F.

How to Locate Muskies

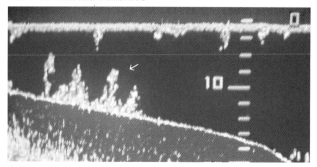

SOUND with a depth finder to locate a reef with thick cabbage (arrow). You can locate a good reef more quickly this way than you can by sight.

LOOK into the water with polarized sunglasses to find the edge of the weeds. Stay away from the edge, but within easy casting distance.

CAST a bucktail over the weeds while motoring along the edge. If you see a swirl or a muskie follows, stop and make another cast or two.

TOSS out a marker if the fish won't strike. Try a couple more spots, then come back a few hours later. The fish may be in a more aggressive mood.

Woman Lake:
Bluegills

During the spawning season, you'll have no trouble finding bluegills on Woman Lake — all you have to do is look. In the clear water, spawning beds appear as round, light-colored depressions. And often you can spot the fish themselves. Most of them run about ½ pound, and you'll catch a few pushing a pound.

Bluegills begin congregating near their spawning areas in mid-May. Some build nests along the shoreline of the main lake, but most spawn in the shallow bays and connecting lakes because the water there warms sooner.

You'll find the spawning beds in vegetation such as wild rice, bulrushes and lily pads. Look for the beds in openings between the weeds, usually at depths of 1 to 3 feet. You'll also find beds in manmade channels and around boat docks. Spawning begins in late May, peaks in mid-June and tapers off by the end of the month.

Fishing is best on warm, sunny days with little or no wind. Under these conditions, you can easily see the beds and the fish are active. They'll bite all day long.

To catch bedding bluegills, all you need is a simple bobber rig baited with a garden worm, waxworm or small leech, but fly-fishing is sportier and at times more effective. You can drop your fly into pockets that would be difficult to reach with a bobber rig. And after you catch a fish, you don't have to spend time baiting up.

For bobber fishing, use an ultralight spinning outfit with 4-pound mono. To reach tight pockets, try a long cane pole or extension pole. For fly-fishing, use a 4- to 5-weight fly rod with floating line, and a 4- to

LURES AND RIGS include (1) Gaines Lightning Bug Popper, (2) Beetle Spin, (3) Alder wet fly, (4) ⅟₃₂-ounce twister tail jig, (5) European-style float, rigged to slip, and a size 8 hook baited with a leech. For ice fishing or open water: (6) teardrop and waxworm.

How to Catch Spawning Bluegills

MOTOR slowly through the lily pads, looking for spawning beds (inset). The commotion may temporarily spook the fish, but they'll return in 5 or 10 minutes.

ANCHOR within casting distance of the beds, then cast with a slip-bobber rig baited with a small leech or use a tiny fly-rod popper. When the action slows, look for some new beds.

Ice Fishing for Bluegills

SPRING-BOBBERS (arrow) help detect subtle bluegill bites in winter. Start your bait near the bottom and jiggle it while lifting your rod. When the spring twitches or stops moving in sync with the rod, set the hook.

8-pound leader. Spawning bluegills aren't fussy; most anglers prefer tiny poppers and wet flies, but any kind of small fly will work.

After spawning, the smaller bluegills remain in the shallow weeds, but the big ones move deeper. You can find them along the deep edges of cabbage beds, usually at depths of 12 to 18 feet. Any cabbage bed will hold a few fish, but the best ones have an irregular edge and are near the spawning areas.

Bobber fishing with live bait works as well in summer as in spring, but the bobber should be rigged to slip so you can reach deeper water. Another option is casting tiny spinnerbaits and twister-tail jigs with an ultralight spinning outfit and 4-pound mono.

Simply drift or slow-troll the edges of cabbage beds until you find the fish.

As in spring, bluegills bite best in calm, sunny weather. You can catch them anytime, but the fastest action comes early or late in the day.

The summer pattern holds up until mid-September. Then the fish begin moving deeper, often into inside

turns along the weed flats. Look for them at depths of 20 feet or more. You'll often find them mixed with crappies, although crappies tend to suspend farther from the weeds. Use the same baits and techniques you would in spring.

After freeze-up, look for bluegills in shallow, weedy bays. They bite best as soon as the ice is safe, and good fishing continues for a couple weeks. The action slows as the ice thickens but picks up again in March and continues to improve until ice-out.

In early and late winter, you'll find most of the fish at depths of 3 to 8 feet; in midwinter, 8 to 20 feet. The secret to catching bluegills in winter is to keep moving until you find them. It pays to keep your hand auger or power auger sharp.

For ice fishing, use a 3-foot jigglestick with 2- to 4-pound mono and a teardrop jig baited with a waxworm or a few Eurolarvae. Attach a small float and set it to keep the bait about a foot off bottom. If the fish are biting lightly or if you prefer to jig at different depths, try a spring-bobber (see photo above) instead of a float fastened to your line.

FISH for the male crappies, which are the darker ones (left), at spawning time. They're much more aggressive than the females (right), and they're quicker to grab a small jig dangled in front of them.

Woman Lake:
Crappies

In Woman Lake, as in many other midwestern walleye lakes, crappies are a mystery fish. Each spring, good numbers of them show up in shallow bays, but then they disappear and few are seen the rest of the open-water season.

Shortly after ice-out, crappies move into weedy, muck-bottomed bays that are several degrees warmer than the main lake. Spawning is still a month away, but crappies are drawn by the plentiful supply of baitfish.

Spawning begins in mid-May, when the water temperature reaches the low 60s. Look for crappies among emergent vegetation, such as bulrushes or cane, growing on a hard bottom. You'll find most of the fish in 2 to 4 feet of water. To spot them, drift or slowly troll over the spawning beds. You may scare the fish away, but they'll return shortly. Carefully mark the spot where you spotted them so you can come back later and fish for them.

After spawning, males stay near the beds to guard the fry for the next week or two. But by early June most of the adults have scattered into deeper water.

To catch crappies around spawning time, use a light spinning outfit with 4- to 6-pound mono, a slip-bobber rig, and a $\frac{1}{16}$- to $\frac{1}{64}$-ounce jig. If the crappies are fussy, replace the jig with a small minnow on a size 4 hook.

Once you spot a crappie, try to put the jig or minnow as close to it as possible. A spawner isn't likely to move very far to take a bait. You may have to dangle it right in front

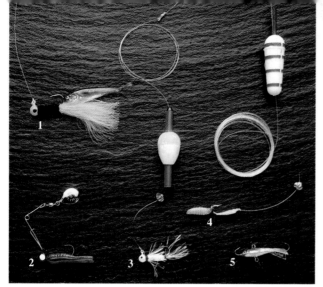

LURES AND RIGS include: (1) marabou jig with minnow, (2) Beetle Spin, (3) bobber rig with Lindy Little Guppy jig. For ice fishing: (4) bobber rig with teardrop jig and waxworm, (5) W-2 Jigging Rapala.

NIGHT FISHING with a small minnow and bobber produces lots of wintertime crappies.

How to Catch Crappies Around Spawning Time

LOOK for crappies in old bulrush beds. The beds aren't as distinct as bluegill beds, but you'll see the fish between the broken-off shoots.

TIE a piece of cloth to an old bulrush shoot where you spot some crappies. They'll move away temporarily, but will return in a few minutes.

CAST a slip-bobber and jig over a bed. Twitch the bobber to give the jig action. Often, the bobber barely moves when a crappie inhales the jig.

of the fish's nose (photo at left). Sometimes the bobber won't even move when a fish bites, but if you watch carefully, you'll see the bait disappear. Set the hook immediately.

During the spawning season, crappies bite all day. Calm, sunny weather is best, although the fish spook more easily under these conditions.

Few Woman Lake anglers bother fishing for crappies in summer and fall, but you can catch them if you know where to look. A sensitive flasher, LCR or video is a big help. Motor along the edges of weedy bars, sunken islands, rock piles and points, looking for telltale marks at depths of 10 to 25 feet. At least some of the crappies in a school will be suspended, so the marks look different from those of walleyes.

Once you find a school, lower a small spinnerbait or a jig and minnow to the proper depth and jig vertically while drifting or slow-trolling. Or still-fish with a slip-bobber rig and minnow. This pattern holds into early fall, but by mid-September, the fish begin moving

deeper. You'll find them in deep holes in the main lake and bays, usually suspended 3 to 10 feet above the bottom in 25 to 35 feet of water. Use the same techniques you would in summer.

After freeze-up, when the ice is thick enough to walk on, look for crappies in the same shallow, weedy areas they frequent in spring and early summer. By midwinter, however, they've moved back to the deep holes where they were in late fall. They return to the shallow, weedy bays just before ice-out.

For ice fishing, use a small bobber with a teardrop-waxworm combination, or a minnow on a plain hook. Or jig with a small Jigging Rapala. A light 2- to 3-foot spinning outfit spooled with 4- to 6-pound mono makes an ideal jigging outfit.

You'll find crappies in water less than 15 feet deep in early and late winter; 30 feet or more in midwinter. They're likely to be suspended. To find them, sound with a flasher or simply change depths periodically by moving your bobber.

Woman Lake:
Smallmouth Bass

While not considered a "numbers" lake, Woman Lake produces some of the region's biggest smallmouths. Each year, anglers take several in the 5- to 6-pound class, and occasionally someone lands one pushing 7.

Most of the big smallies are caught in spring, just after the season opens in late May or early June. In a normal spring, the opener falls near the spawning peak.

Smallmouths are easy to find during the spawning period. On a calm day, put on a pair of polarized sunglasses and drift or motor slowly over a shallow rocky reef. If the fish are there, you'll see them.

The most productive reefs are 3 to 10 feet deep and connected to shore. The bottom consists of sand, gravel and a mixture of softball- to basketball-sized boulders.

When you find the fish, keep your boat a short distance away and cast to them. In water this shallow and clear, trolling over the fish will probably spook them. A surface lure such as a small propbait works well in calm weather, especially early and late in the day. On windy days, you'll do better with a small crankbait, a tube jig, or a slip-bobber rig baited with a leech.

The males stay in the same areas for a week or two after spawning and can still be caught on jigs, crankbaits and propbaits. The females, which are larger, may drop into water as deep as 18 feet. They're often finicky so you may have to use live bait. At these depths, you can troll over the fish using a quiet electric motor and a slip-sinker rig baited with a leech, nightcrawler or shiner.

For fishing propbaits and crankbaits, carry a medium-power baitcasting outfit with 8-pound mono; for jigs, slip-bobber rigs and slip-sinker rigs, a light- to medium-power spinning outfit with 6-pound mono.

Once the fish abandon their spawning areas and move deeper, they're much tougher to find. During the summer, walleye anglers catch an occasional smallmouth by accident, but the fish are too scattered to catch consistently.

By late August, however, smallmouths begin to bunch up along the breaks of rocky reefs projecting from the shoreline or from Horseshoe Island. Most of them relate to points along the breakline that drop gradually into water at least 35 feet deep.

In early fall, you'll find the fish at depths of 15 to 25 feet, but as the water cools, they go deeper. By late September, most of them retreat to depths of 30 to 40 feet. They school more tightly as the season progresses. A good graph can be a big help in locating them.

Fall fishermen commonly use a slip-sinker rig baited with a 3- to 4-inch redtail chub. With winter coming, the fish feed heavily and seem to prefer larger baits than in spring or summer. Often these big baits produce a bonus walleye or northern pike.

During most of the year, smallmouths bite best on overcast days with a slight chop, preferably after a period of stable weather. You'll probably catch more fish in the morning and evening than in midday. In late fall, however, the reverse is true. Fishing is best on sunny, Indian summer days, with the fastest bite right in the middle of the day.

LURES AND RIGS for smallmouths include: (1) slip-sinker rig with a size 2 hook and a 3- to 4-inch redtail chub, (2) 1/16-ounce tube jig, (3) slip-bobber rig with a size 4 hook and a leech; (4) Bill Lewis Rat-L-Top propbait, (5) Floating Rapala, (6) Poe's Series 1100 crankbait.

How to Twitch a Minnow Plug for Smallmouths

CAST a floating minnow plug into the shallows and let it rest until the ripples subside. Some anglers wait as long as a minute.

RETRIEVE with a series of sharp twitches, keeping the lure on the surface. It should dart to the side, hesitate, then dart to the other side.

WATCH carefully or you may miss subtle strikes. Often a fish barely noses the lure, as if pushing it out of the way.

If you see the lure twitch or move unexpectedly, set the hook immediately.

Woman Lake:
Largemouth Bass

You'll seldom catch a largemouth in the main body of Woman Lake, but there are plenty of them in its shallow bays and connecting lakes, including a few that tip the scales at 7 pounds or more.

In the main lake, the vegetation is too sparse to hold many largemouths. The bays, however, have thicker vegetation and warmer water. Bays with only a narrow connection to the main lake hold the most bass. If the connection is too wide, the bays attract few bass in spring because the wind blows in water from the lake, greatly reducing the water temperature.

Like smallmouths, largemouths bite best early in the season. Their springtime activity centers mainly around spawning. Depending on the progress of the season, they may be in a prespawn, spawning or postspawn mode when the season opens in late May or early June.

In an early spring, most fish have completed spawning by the opener. But in a late spring, they're still on the beds and highly vulnerable. They're easy to see, and will hit almost anything tossed their way. Look for the beds in 1 to 5 feet of water around sunken logs, lily pad roots, or old mats of vegetation. You'll also find beds in bulrushes, beaver trenches and man-made boat canals.

By mid-June, the new vegetation becomes thick enough to provide overhead cover. Bass move into the "slop," where the water is slightly cooler and the young, as well as the adults, are protected from predators. On Woman Lake, this heavy, matted vegetation consists mainly of lily pads and wild rice, with a mixture of submerged plants.

Before the slop develops, spinnerbaits, weightless worms or topwater lures such as buzzbaits or stickbaits are the best choice. When the slop really gets thick, you'll need a totally weedless lure, such as a rubber frog, Texas-rigged plastic worm or weedless spoon. Carry a medium-heavy 7-foot flippin' stick with 17-pound mono for casting buzzbaits, spinnerbaits and weedless spoons; a medium-heavy 5½-foot baitcasting outfit with 12-pound mono for the other lures.

Once the slop develops, the pattern changes very little through late September. The fish move way up into the thickest slop on sunny days, and they cruise the outside edges of the weeds on cloudy days, but they're never far from the heavy vegetation.

LURES include: (1) Zara Puppy stickbait, (2) Snag Proof Frog, (3) 4-inch ring worm, (4) 6-inch Producto Worm, (5) Moss Boss weedless spoon, (6) ⅜-ounce J-Mac jig and Guido Bug, (7) Blue Fox spinnerbait, (8) Bill Norman Triple-Winged Buzzbait, (9) Bomber Fat A crankbait, (10) Slug-Go worm.

Docks also hold a lot of bass in summer and early fall. Bass prefer docks in water at least 3 feet deep and near the inside weedline; with the weeds this close, the fish can easily move back and forth.

The techniques for bass in summer and early fall are much the same as those used after the slop develops in spring. But when bass are in the deeper wild rice, try a jig-and-pig or a 4-inch Texas-rigged plastic worm. These lures will penetrate small crevices in the rice to reach the bass that lie below.

By early October, the slop has deteriorated. It will still hold a few bass, but most of them seek cover in deeper, submerged weeds. Look for the greenest weeds you can find, which will usually be coontail, and fish along the outside weedline at a depth of 10 to 14 feet.

Weedline bass usually hold in tight schools, so if you can find them, you'll have some fast fishing. Effective late-fall lures include a jig-and-pig, a ½-ounce spinnerbait and a deep-diving crankbait.

Bass feed most heavily on warm, overcast days with little or no wind, particularly if the weather has been stable for several days. Although slop bass may bite any time of the day, mornings and evenings are generally best. In late fall, bass activity gradually increases through the day as the water warms.

How to Catch Largemouths in Slop

CAST a weedless spoon into the slop; keep your rod tip high and retrieve slowly so the spoon slides over the weeds. Pause when it comes to an opening and let it flutter down (inset). If a bass hits, set the hook and lift to keep the fish out of the thick vegetation.

SLIDE the bass over the slop while holding its head up. If you let the fish dive, it may wrap around a weed and shake the hook. A flippin' stick with heavy mono (at least 17-pound test) is a must to get enough upward pull to keep the fish on top of the weeds.

CAST "with the grain" of the wild rice so your lure stays in the slots. If you retrieve across the grain, your lure is much more likely to foul.

EQUIP your push pole with a duckbill to move your boat through heavy slop. Tip your outboard up so it doesn't drag in the weeds.

BUZZ weeds off your trolling motor by lifting it out of the water and spinning the prop at high speed. A weed-cutter prop (inset) reduces weed buildup.

ADD a trailer hook if you're getting short strikes on a weedless spoon. Slide a piece of surgical tubing over the eye of the trailer, then push the trailer over the main hook.

CARRY several pre-rigged rods; when you want to fish a different type of cover, such as a dock or an opening or edge in the slop, you don't have to change lures.

Woman Lake:

Northern Pike

Many Woman Lake anglers, especially the muskie enthusiasts, have little time for northern pike. Because northerns hatch earlier in the spring than muskies, young pike prey on the smaller muskie fry.

Those who enjoy pike fishing, however, know that the lake has a good population of 4- to 6-pounders and occasionally produces a 15- to 20-pounder.

Northerns bite best when the water is cool. From mid-May to early June, look for them on shallow, rocky reefs with developing weeds. As the water warms, however, the larger pike move away from the shallow, weedy areas and are difficult to find. They return to the shallows when the water cools, usually in mid-September, and fishing is good through mid-October.

Fishermen using medium-heavy spinning or bait-casting gear with 10- to 14-pound mono catch plenty of pike on good-sized spoons, bucktails, jerkbaits or jigs tipped with 4- to 6-inch minnows. Some anglers prefer to use muskie gear (p. 95) for big pike lures. Suckers from 6 to 10 inches long, fished beneath a large slip-bobber, also take a lot of pike.

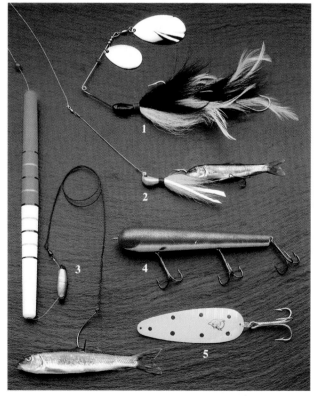

LURES AND RIGS include: (1) Lindy Giant Tandem Spin, (2) ½-ounce Northland Sting'r Bucktail Jig and sucker, (3) slip-bobber rig with 20-pound wire leader, size 2/0 hook and sucker, (4) Eddie Bait, (5) Dardevle.

Woman Lake:
Yellow Perch

With the smorgasbord of gamefish in Woman Lake, few anglers pay much attention to yellow perch. But if you're looking for a change of pace, the lake holds plenty of "jumbos." They average about half a pound, but some are more than twice that size.

Most perch are caught by ice fishermen. The fish bite all winter long, but the prime time is the month before ice-out. Look for the fish off the sides of points and bars, not right on the drop-off, usually at depths of 25 to 35 feet.

Using a light 3-foot rod and a small spinning reel spooled with 4-pound mono, lower a ⅛-ounce jig or Swedish Pimple tipped with a minnow, part of a minnow or a perch eye to the bottom. Work the lure with short lifts followed by long pauses. Perch usually bite after the lure comes to rest.

Another good ice-fishing technique: remove the hook from a Swedish Pimple or jigging spoon, and attach a short 6-pound mono dropper with a size 6 hook (photo at upper right). Bait the hook with a perch eye, waxworm or minnow head. The lure provides enough weight to get down quickly, and its flash draws perch to the bait.

Early summer is the next best time to catch perch. In June, they feed heavily on minnows around the ends of shallow sand-gravel points, especially those with sandgrass on the bottom. With a light spinning outfit and 4-pound mono, cast a slip-sinker and minnow rig or a ⅛-ounce jig and minnow into 8 to 10 feet of water on top of the point and work it down the slope.

LURES AND RIGS for Woman Lake perch include: (1) ⅛-ounce Fuzz-E-Grub tipped with a minnow, (2) ⅛-ounce Mister Twister Meeny jig, (3) slip-sinker rig with a ⅛-ounce sinker and a size 6 hook baited with a minnow. For ice fishing: (4) Swedish Pimple with minnow.

Bass-Panfish Lakes

These fertile farm-country lakes produce more fish than any other type of natural lake

If you're looking for seclusion and picturebook scenery, you won't find them on the typical bass-panfish lake. Although some of these lakes are surrounded by undeveloped woodlands, most are found in agricultural regions or heavily populated areas. But for anglers who aren't into aesthetics, these lakes have a lot to offer.

Most bass-panfish lakes are eutrophic. Runoff carries in nutrients from cities and farm fields, causing heavy growths of plankton, which result in an abundance of food. Consequently, these lakes can support more and faster-growing fish than lakes with lower nutrient levels.

High nutrient levels also cause lush growths of aquatic vegetation. In extremely fertile lakes, however, the plankton becomes so thick it keeps sunlight from reaching the bottom, preventing plants from taking root.

The basins of these lakes are so shallow that the water gets very warm in summer. Although a thermocline may form, there is seldom enough oxygen in the depths to sustain gamefish. As a result, they're found in shallow water most of the time.

Because of the warm water and dense weed growth, bass and panfish are the dominant gamefish species. The silty bottoms and periodic oxygen sags allow roughfish, especially bullheads and carp, to gain a foothold.

Many of these lakes also support northern pike and walleyes. As a rule, the walleyes must be stocked; there is not enough clean rubble bottom for successful spawning.

Even though gamefish may be plentiful, they're seldom easy to catch. The abundant supply of food means that feeding periods tend to be short. And the thick, weedy cover makes it difficult to get your bait to the fish.

The best time to fish these lakes is in spring, before the heavy weed growth develops. Food is least abundant in spring, too, so the fish must spend more of

their time feeding. Fishing usually slows in summer, after the weeds develop and young-of-the-year forage fish grow large enough to interest the gamefish. The action picks up again in fall after the weeds die back and a good share of the young forage fish have been eaten.

Some of these lakes, particularly the shallower ones, suffer winterkills in years of heavy snow cover,

especially if the snow comes early. Gamefish die from lack of oxygen. If winterkills are too frequent, the lake becomes dominated by roughfish, which can better tolerate low oxygen levels.

To alleviate the problem, some natural resources agencies have installed aeration systems to agitate the water and restore oxygen. Many aerated lakes now offer outstanding fishing.

Case Study:

Big Round Lake, Wisconsin

Like thousands of other bass-panfish lakes around the country, Big Round was formed when a glacial ice block melted (p. 9). Over time, the lake has become much shallower as sediment has filled in most of the original basin and obscured all but a few irregularities on the bottom. As its name suggests, the lake has a rounded shape, although there are a few subtle bays and points.

The lake is fed by the Straight River, a small stream draining farmland to the northwest. The stream carries in nutrients from the heavily fertilized fields, resulting in a "pea-soup" algae bloom in summer.

Despite the high fertility level and a maximum depth of only 17 feet, Big Round has never frozen out. The river carries in enough oxygenated water to prevent winterkill even in years of heavy snow cover.

Because the lake is so shallow and the basin so exposed to the wind, the water mixes from top to bottom and no thermocline forms in summer. After a few hot, still days, however, the bottom is usually a few degrees cooler than the surface.

Round is clearer than most eutrophic lakes, with a Secchi disk reading of 5 to 6 feet most of the year. In

midsummer, however, the reading dips to about a foot because of the heavy algae bloom.

The shoreline and shallows of Big Round are primarily sand or a sand-gravel mix, but the main basin is silt and muck. Large stands of bulrushes grow in the shallows, and thick beds of coontail, milfoil and cabbage flourish down to a depth of 8 feet.

As in most lakes of this type, largemouth bass are the dominant predator fish, and there are healthy populations of panfish, in this case, bluegills, black crappies and perch. The perch run small, but they make excellent forage.

Walleyes are stocked regularly in Big Round, and there's a remnant population of muskies, the result of past stockings. Although few anglers intentionally fish for muskies in Big Round, the lake produced a 50-pound, 4-ouncer in 1989. You may catch an occasional good-sized northern pike, but there aren't enough of them to generate much interest among anglers.

Although Big Round has no resorts, there are more than 100 private cabins, so fishing pressure is quite heavy. The lake's reputation for good bass fishing and wintertime walleye fishing also draws anglers from the surrounding area.

Big Round Lake Physical Data

Acreage	1,015
Average depth	10 ft
Maximum depth	17 ft
Clarity	1 to 6 ft
Color	green
Total phosphorus (parts per billion)	120
Thermocline	none
Average date of freeze-up	December 1
Average date of ice-out	April 14

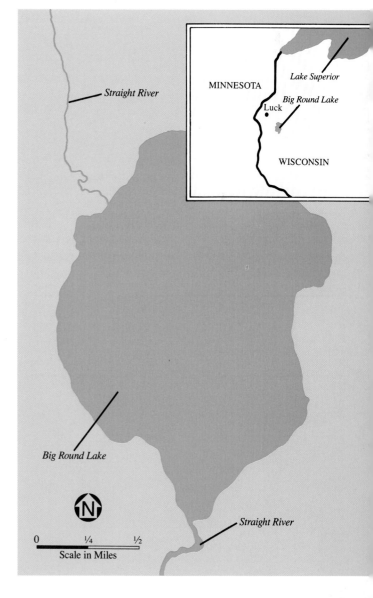

Straight River

MINNESOTA

Lake Superior

Big Round Lake

Luck

WISCONSIN

Big Round Lake

Straight River

0   ¼   ½
Scale in Miles

Round Lake Habitat *(sample locations of habitats are marked on NASA photo)*

1. BULRUSH BEDS draw bass, bluegills, crappies and walleyes in spring and fall. The deepest beds hold some bass through the summer.

2. LILY PADS grow on a dark, mucky bottom, and the water around them warms rapidly in spring, attracting prespawn largemouths.

3. BARS AND FLATS in midlake attract walleyes most of the year. Bass, bluegills and crappies use the bars and flats in summer and winter.

4. DOCKS, especially the deepest ones, hold largemouths and bluegills from summer through early fall. Docks are best in normal to high water.

5. BAYS, though not deeply indented from the rest of the shoreline, warm quickly in spring, so bass, bluegills and crappies move in to spawn.

6. POINTS in the outside weedline hold bass in summer and walleyes in early winter. Follow the margin of the matted weeds to find the points.

NASA High Altitude Photograph →

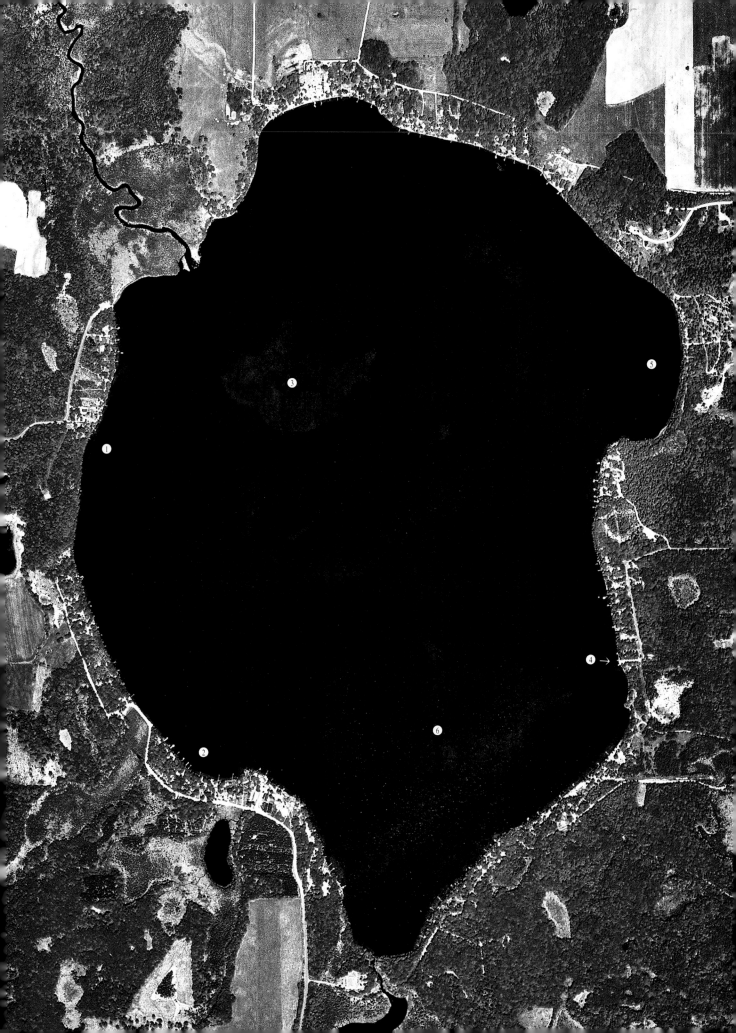

Big Round Lake:

Largemouth Bass

The shallow, weed-choked waters of Big Round are heaven for largemouth bass. Better known for numbers than size, the lake has hordes of 11- to 13-inchers. On a good day, you can catch two or three dozen, along with a few 2- to 3-pounders. And there's an outside chance of connecting with a 5- to 7-pounder. Largemouths start to feed heavily in mid-May, about two weeks before they spawn. You can find them almost anyplace in the shallows where there are old bulrushes or lily pads, or new growths of coontail or cabbage.

The main draw this time of year is warm water. If you have a temperature gauge, motor along the shoreline and look for warmwater zones. Usually, the bays have the warmest water and draw the most bass. If the water temperature is below 50° F, the fish probably won't be in the shallows.

Another attraction in late spring is spawning sunfish. If you can find a colony of spawning beds, you're likely to find the bass. They move in to feed on

How to Work Matted Weeds

TOSS a jig-and-pig or a Texas-rigged plastic worm on top of a dense weed mat. Hold your rod tip high as you retrieve so the lure slides over the weeds. Sometimes bass come out of the weeds and grab the lure on the surface.

PAUSE and lower your rod tip when the jig reaches the edge of the weeds or comes to a pocket. Be sure to keep the line taut as the jig sinks so you can feel the fish strike. Set the hook immediately.

How to Skip a Worm Under a Dock

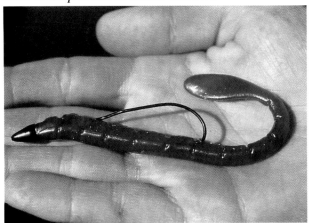

SELECT a fat-bodied worm; the broader surface makes it skip better than a skinnier worm. Rig the worm Texas style and peg the sinker so it doesn't separate from the worm when you cast.

SKIP the worm into the shadiest area under a dock. Using a spinning outfit with 10-pound mono, cast the worm with a sharp sidearm motion so it lands close to the dock, then skips underneath.

crayfish, minnows and other sunfish-egg predators, as well as on the sunfish themselves.

To locate springtime bass, use a shallow-running lure that allows you to cover water quickly, such as a ¼-ounce tandem spinnerbait. In morning or evening or under other dim-light conditions, try a ¼- to ⅜-ounce buzzbait or a propbait fished with a reel-and-pause retrieve. When you locate some fish and want to work the area more thoroughly, switch to a ¼-ounce jig-and-pig.

In spring, largemouths bite best from midafternoon to dusk, the period of highest water temperature. You'll catch the most fish on warm, still, cloudy days, especially after several days of warm, stable weather. Sunny days with a light breeze can be good too.

By mid-June, the water temperature has risen into the 70s and the weeds are almost fully developed. Under bright conditions, look for bass right in the thickest submerged weedbeds or in the shadiest areas under docks. In low-light conditions, you'll find bass in openings in the weeds, on points along the outside weedlines, and around the docks. A few bass remain in the deeper bulrushes.

Use a buzzbait to "call up" bass in the thick weeds; or work a jig-and-pig or Texas-rigged plastic worm through the weeds and along the weedline. Fish the docks with a fat-bodied plastic worm.

When the water greens up during an algae bloom, many of the bass in deep water move shallower. The blanket of algae is so thick it provides shade.

LURES for largemouths include: (1) ¼-ounce Arkie Jig with a crawfrog, (2) single-spin spinnerbait with a curly-tail grub, (3) ⅜-ounce J-Mac Jig with a jumbo pork frog, (4) Fleck Spinnerbait with a curly-tail grub, (5) Northland Buzz-ard with a curly-tail grub, (6) Culprit Worm, Texas rigged with a ³⁄₁₆-ounce bullet sinker, (7) Producto Worm, Texas rigged with a pegged ¹⁄₁₆-ounce bullet sinker, (8) A.C. Shiner 00, (9) Devil's Horse.

Summertime bass bite best in the same type of weather as in spring. Morning and evening fishing is most productive, especially when you're working the dense weeds; the bass move out of the thick mats and feed along the edges.

By late September, most of the shallow submerged weeds have died. Many bass move into deep clumps of green coontail, although you'll find some in the deeper bulrush beds, particularly those nearest the edge of the break.

Work the edges of a bulrush patch with a ¼- to ⅜-ounce jig-and-pig, occasionally casting back into the rushes to catch less active bass. Use a jig-and-pig, a ½-ounce single-spin spinnerbait or a medium-diving crankbait to fish the deeper coontail clumps.

Through most of the fall, fishing is best in cloudy weather, just as in spring and summer. But starting in early October, largemouths bite better on sunny, Indian summer days, often right in midafternoon.

Because of the dense weeds in Big Round, most anglers use medium-heavy baitcasting outfits, 5½ to 6 feet long, with 12- to 20-pound mono, depending on the cover. For worm fishing, carry a 6-foot, medium-heavy spinning outfit with 10-pound mono.

Anyone can catch small bass on Big Round, but the big ones are hard to come by. Small bass race after any lure that comes by. The big bass are lazy; they hold tighter to cover and aren't anxious to go out of their way to get food. If they ignore a fast-moving buzzbait, for instance, try slowly retrieving a jig-and-pig in or alongside the weeds.

A jig-and-pig is a good choice for big bass

"Pitchin' " a Jig-and-Pig in the Bulrushes

1. REDUCE your spool tension by loosening the adjustment knob. The spool must turn freely in order to get enough distance when you pitch the jig.

2. ANGLE your rod tip downward, push the thumb bar, and thumb the spool. Hold the jig with your other hand so there is slight tension between the jig and the rod.

3. PITCH the jig toward a pocket in the weeds using a smooth, upward, shoveling motion; at the same time, release the jig.

4. STOP the jig in the exact spot by thumbing the spool. The jig should set down gently. With practice, you should be able to pitch 30 feet with good accuracy.

Tips for Catching Bass in Fertile Lakes

SWITCH to a larger pork chunk when bass refuse to strike your jig-and-pig. The bulkier pork keeps your jig on top of the weeds, and when the jig reaches a hole, it will sink more slowly, giving bass extra time to strike.

SELECT a plastic worm with metallic flecks when fishing in low-clarity water. The flecks reflect light in different directions, so there's a better chance that largemouths will notice the worm.

Big Round Lake:

Walleyes

Thanks to an intensive stocking program, Big Round holds a surprising number of walleyes. The fish cannot reproduce naturally; the soft, weedy bottom makes poor spawning habitat.

Most of the fish run 1½ to 3 pounds, and anglers catch a few 8- to 10-pounders each year. The lake record is 13.

The dense weed growth and plentiful food supply make walleye fishing in Big Round a challenge. Your best chances are in May, before the weeds become too thick and the new crop of young perch reach eating size, or after first ice in December.

When the season opens in early May, look for walleyes along the outside margins of bulrush beds or on the hard-bottomed midlake bars. You'll find them at depths ranging from 2 to 10 feet, usually where there's new-growth coontail or milfoil on the bottom.

To catch early-season walleyes in dim-light conditions, cast or troll a shallow-running minnow plug or crankbait over the shallowest part of the structure. In bright conditions, cast a jig and minnow or a deep-diving crankbait along the sides. Use a 6-foot medium-power spinning outfit with 6-pound mono.

Because the water is quite clear in spring, walleyes bite best early or late in the day or at night. Cloud cover or a light chop improves fishing.

By early July, walleyes start moving into the newly developed weeds to find cover and shade. They're tough to catch, although you can take a few by slow-trolling a slip-sinker rig tight to the weedline on the midlake bars, usually at a depth of about 8 feet. Or

you can toss a slip-bobber rig into pockets in the weeds or up against the weedline. Leeches are the favorite of most local anglers.

During heavy summertime algae blooms, water clarity decreases so much that walleyes begin feeding in midday. When the bloom subsides, they go back to their normal morning and evening pattern.

By late September, many of the submerged weeds have died off. Baitfish move into the bulrushes and the walleyes follow. Look for them along the outside edges of bulrush beds, in depths of 3 to 10 feet. Use the same techniques as in spring. Walleyes continue to bite until freeze-up.

Big Round has a reputation as an outstanding winter walleye lake, and anglers start fishing as soon as the ice is safe. In early winter, look for the fish on points in the outside weedline, usually at depths of about 10 feet. Later, fish the edges of midlake bars at depths of 10 to 12 feet.

Tip-up fishing with 3- to 5-inch minnows, preferably golden shiners, is the most popular way to catch Round Lake walleyes in winter, but jigging may work even better.

Walleyes bite best from 3 to 9 p.m. Ice fishing holds up well until mid-January, but then the action slows until mid- to late February.

The ice fishing season closes on March 1.

Jigging lures often outfish minnows

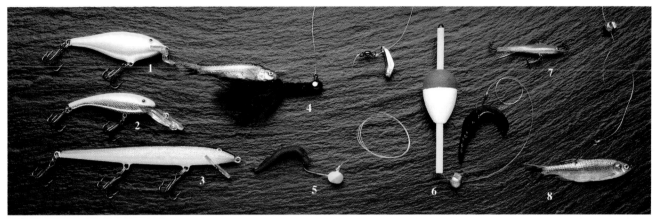

LURES AND RIGS include: (1) Shallow Shad Rap, (2) Cordell Wally Diver, (3) Floating Rapala, (4) ¼-ounce jig and minnow, (5) slip-sinker rig with Northland Float'n Jig Head and leech, (6) slip-bobber rig with size 4 hook and leech. For ice fishing: (7) W-5 Jigging Rapala, (8) size 4 hook and shiner for use with tip-up.

Tips for Catching Weed Walleyes

SELECT a weedless jig with the attachment eye at the nose. An ordinary ball-head weedless jig doesn't work as well; weeds gather in front of the eye (inset) rather than slide around the head.

USE a bullet sinker when fishing a slip-sinker rig through the weeds. The tapered sinker will not pick up bits of weeds as a standard walking sinker will.

WORK the edges of a weedy bar or flat using a slip-bobber rig baited with a leech. Walleyes take cover in the weeds, but the wiggling leech will draw them out.

Try ice flies or teardrops tipped with grubs in summer as well as winter

Big Round Lake:

Bluegills

The 'gills in Big Round aren't huge, but they'll give you a good tussle on ultralight spinning gear. They average 2 or 3 to the pound, and you'll catch a few weighing ¾ pound or a little better.

Ice-out is normally in mid-April, and as soon as the water warms a few degrees, bluegills move into the shallows. You'll find them in water from 6 inches to 4 feet deep, wherever there are dead weeds. The water is clear enough then that you should be able to see the fish if you wear polarized sunglasses. When you find a concentration, cast to them with a tiny float and a small leech or piece of garden worm.

Around spawning time, from late May to late June, you can catch bluegills as fast as you can get your line in the water — if you can find a colony of spawning beds. Check out any openings in the newly emerging bulrushes, or in the shallow submerged weeds; they're often a tip-off to the location of a spawning colony.

If you find a colony, try a tiny jig, about ¹⁄₆₄ ounce, instead of live bait. The fish are so aggressive that the type of bait doesn't really matter, and a jig allows you to get your line back in the water in a hurry without taking time to bait up. With a jig this small, you'll need a bobber for casting weight. Use a slip-bobber instead of an ordinary bobber when fishing in bulrushes; the bobber and jig are closer together, so the rig is less likely to tangle around the stems when you cast.

After spawning, small bluegills stay in shallow water, but the big ones go deeper. They congregate along the weedlines of midlake bars at a depth of 8 to 10 feet. Set a slip-bobber to the right depth, bait up with a small leech or a piece of one, and cast to the edge of the weeds. Keep the rig as tight to the weedline as possible. Don't be surprised if you catch a walleye or a bass while you're at it.

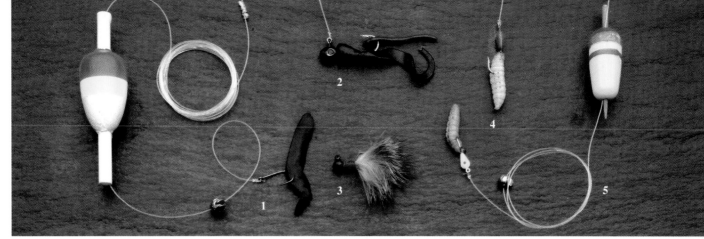

LURES AND RIGS: (1) slip-bobber rig with size 8 hook and small leech, (2) $\frac{1}{32}$-ounce jig and piece of worm, (3) $\frac{1}{64}$-ounce hair jig, (4) tullibee hook and waxworm. For ice fishing: (5) bobber rig with ice fly and waxworm.

Tips for Finding Bluegills

CHECK sparse pockets (dotted line) along the weedline for bluegills. The lighter weed growth often results from harder bottom materials.

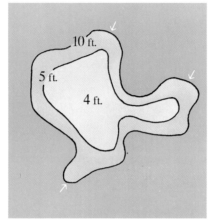

LOOK for bluegills on sharp points (arrows) projecting from midlake flats. The points are especially important in summer and winter.

DROP a bobber rig baited with a worm or small leech into openings in the bulrushes, where bluegills often build their nests.

Midlake bars produce through the summer, but when the water begins to cool in early September, bluegills move back toward shore. Check deep, outside weedlines in the bays and just out from bulrush beds. Tip a $\frac{1}{32}$-ounce jig with a small leech, waxworm or piece of garden worm. Cast it along the weedline, ticking it over the weedtops. Later in September, many of the fish move into 15-foot holes and anglers catch them on the same baits as in early fall.

The lake freezes up around December 1, and as soon as the ice is safe, try working 6- to 8-foot weed flats in the bays. In January, move to the midlake bars and look for the fish in about 10 feet of water, just off the edges or on projecting points. Remember that the fish may be suspended. Using a noodle rod (photo at right) or a jigglestick equipped with a spring-bobber, lower a teardrop tipped with a waxworm to the bottom, then jig it upward until you find the fish.

Regardless of the season, bluegills will bite any time of day, but you won't catch many after sunset. Stable weather usually means fast action.

ICE FISH for bluegills using a "noodle" rod. The super-soft tip makes it possible to detect subtle strikes without a spring-bobber.

Big Round Lake:
Crappies

Big Round is known as a boom-or-bust crappie lake. Like most lakes with lots of crappies, its population is cyclical. Every five to seven years, the lake produces a bumper crop of crappies, which must compete with each other for food. They grow slowly the first two or three years, during which time anglers catch smaller-than-normal fish. Once the population is thinned down, the remaining fish grow a lot faster and anglers catch much bigger, though considerably fewer, crappies.

Soon after the ice goes out, crappies move into shallow, dark-bottomed bays where the water is slightly warmer. The bays on Big Round aren't very distinct, but they still warm up faster than the rest of the lake.

You can catch springtime crappies on the usual bobber-and-minnow rig, but there's really no need for bait; you'll take just as many on a plain $1/32$-ounce jig fished beneath a small float. For maximum sport, use a 5-foot ultralight spinning out-fit with 4-pound mono.

When the water warms to the low 60s, about the second week in May, crappies move into the old, broken-off bulrushes to spawn. On a calm day, you should be able to

CATCH spawning crappies among the old bulrushes (the broken-off weeds in the background). All you need is a small jig and a bobber.

LURES AND RIGS include: (1) slip-bobber rig with size 4 hook and minnow, (2) $1/32$-ounce Tiny Tube jig, (3) $1/16$-ounce chenille jig. For ice fishing: (4) bobber rig with an ice fly and minnow, or (5) size 8 hook and minnow.

see them if you wear polarized sunglasses. They use the same bulrush beds each year.

During the spawning period, crappies will bite all day, although the action is fastest from late afternoon to dusk. A warming trend usually means good fishing, but strong winds will drive the fish out of the bulrush beds.

Spawning continues for 10 days to two weeks, depending on how fast the water warms. Males stay around a little longer to guard the nests, but by early June, most of the fish have moved out to the edge of shoreline breaks or to the midlake bars. They move around a lot in summer, and they often suspend, so they may be hard to find. As a rule, they're close to the bars or on top of them in cloudy weather; farther off in sunny weather.

Jigs work just as well in summer as in spring, but you'll need heavier ones, about $1/16$ ounce, and no float. Just cast out and work the jig over the weedtops.

Crappies hang around the bars well into fall, but by late September, you'll find them in 10 to 14 feet of water off the bars or on shoreline breaks just outside bulrush beds. Use a $1/16$- to $1/8$-ounce jig or a small minnow on a split-shot rig.

After the lake freezes over, you can still catch crappies in the same spots as in late fall. But by midwinter, most of them have moved away from shore into the deepest holes where they often suspend several feet above the bottom.

All you need for crappies in winter is a jigglestick with 4-pound mono, a small bobber, and a $1\frac{1}{2}$-inch minnow on a plain hook or teardrop. Pinch on enough split shot so the bobber barely floats.

Crappies bite best the first few weeks after freeze-up and the last few weeks before ice-out. Start fishing at dusk; you'll catch fish for a couple hours after dark.

Tips for Catching Crappies

LOOK for crappies on points (dotted line) along the weedline. Sometimes the fish will suspend just out from the weeds. Cast to them with a small jig or spinnerbait (see below).

SLOW-TROLL for crappies along the edges of midlake bars and flats using a curly-tail jig or a small spinnerbait (see below). Stay close to the weeds in sunny weather; farther away when it's cloudy.

PREVENT fouling in dense weeds by using a tiny spinnerbait. The lure's safety-pin design helps protect the exposed hook.

USE a portable flasher to determine how deep to fish in winter. It's possible to find crappies suspended at practically any depth.

Florida Bass Lakes

The promise of a 10-pounder draws bass anglers from all over the country to Florida's lake region

Among the "snowbirds" that migrate southward each winter are tens of thousands of northern anglers eager to sample Florida's renowned bass lakes.

Most northerners have heard about Florida's famous natural lakes — Okeechobee, Kissimmee, Orange-Lochloosa and possibly several others. But few realize that the state has thousands of natural lakes, 7,783 to be exact.

Many have the mistaken idea that Florida's lakes are all shallow, swampy and weed choked. While quite a few fit that category, others are deep and clear with only a narrow fringe of shoreline vegetation. Although 90 percent of the lakes are small (less than 20 acres), some are huge. Okeechobee, the state's largest lake, covers 690 square miles.

Florida's natural lakes fall into three major categories: solution lakes, lakes formed in old seabed depressions, and riverine lakes.

Solution lakes formed when surface or groundwater seeped through and dissolved underground limestone, creating cavities that eventually collapsed and filled with water (p. 11). Also called "sinkhole" lakes, solution lakes normally have a round, cone-shaped basin

Florida bass reach mammoth size, as this 15-pounder proves

with no inlet or outlet. Most are small (less than 250 acres) and deep (more than 25 feet).

Florida's natural lake region is an uplifted seabed, and some of the lake basins are simply depressions in the old sea bottom. These lakes are larger and shallower than solution lakes, and their bottoms are usually flatter. Florida's riverine lakes include oxbows (p. 10) and lakes that are actually wide, shallow portions of rivers.

Although most Florida lakes have the greenish to brownish color typical of highly fertile lakes, about two-thirds of the lakes have low to moderate fertility, so they are not as productive as widely believed. The deepest solution lakes are the least fertile.

Water clarity varies widely, but in most lakes is 5 feet or less. In a few lakes, however, clarity exceeds 25 feet. Florida's spring lakes are among the clearest in the world.

The allure of Florida's lakes stems mainly from a fish that inhabits them, the Florida bass. A subspecies of largemouth bass, the Florida bass grows considerably larger than its northern cousin. Northern largemouth seldom exceed 10 pounds; Floridas may surpass 20.

Not all bass that live in Florida lakes are purebred Florida bass, however. There are "intergrades" between northern and Florida largemouths, and even taxonomists have difficulty determining whether a

126

given specimen is a pure Florida or an intergrade. To anglers, it doesn't really matter. The intergrades seem to get just as big. In fact, many believe that the current world-record largemouth, a 22-pound 4-ounce giant, was an intergrade.

But Florida bass aren't the only attraction. Many of the lakes have black crappies, or "speckled perch" as they're often called; redear sunfish, or "shellcrackers"; bluegills; chain pickerel and even channel catfish. Some lakes are stocked with striped bass and some with striped bass-white bass hybrids, called "sunshine bass."

Because of the year-round growing season, most of the fish in Florida lakes grow faster than their northern counterparts. But they don't live as long, so they aren't necessarily larger.

The fishing season in Florida stays open all year, but angling pressure is heaviest in late winter and early spring, when there are more fishermen around and the bass are concentrated in spawning areas.

There's one major difference in fishing Florida lakes versus lakes in the northern part of the country. Because the water temperature in Florida lakes seldom drops below 55° F in winter, the spring warm-up is more gradual than in northern lakes.

Consequently, all fish species spawn over a much longer period. Largemouths, for example, complete spawning in a week or two in northern lakes. But in Florida, spawning may last as long as four months. Some bass may be spawning while others have finished and moved back to their normal haunts. Still others have not yet started to spawn. As a result of this pattern, you'll find bass scattered over a wide range of habitat, even though spawning is under way.

While Florida lakes offer many outstanding fishing opportunities, a number of waters face serious problems. Florida's population explosion, combined with rapid industrial and agricultural expansion, has led to dramatic increases in the amount of organic pollutants entering some lakes. Algae blooms have increased, causing diminished growth of the rooted aquatic plants that gamefish require for cover. In a few lakes, bass have almost disappeared.

As the human population grows, more and more gamefish spawning and rearing areas are destroyed. Developers fill in wetlands to build homes, and property owners cover shoreline vegetation with sand to make swimming beaches.

Anyone who has driven through Florida and crossed dozens of man-made canals knows the practice of channelization runs rampant in the state. Many canals, supposedly built for flood control, are a guise to drain bottomland for property development. Some

A maze of drainage canals covers some parts of Florida

lakes have lost more than half of their surface area because of drainage.

Water-control devices on the canals are intended to maintain lake levels. But most lakes are now being held at a lower level than in years past. The lower water leads to increased plant growth. When the plants die, decomposition produces sediments that fill in and shrink the lake basin at a faster-than-normal rate.

Compounding this problem is the rapid spread of exotic plants, particularly hydrilla and water hyacinth. Besides further increasing the sedimentation rate, exotics can choke a lake to the point where boat travel is nearly impossible. And they often crowd out the native plants.

In some lakes, however, the invasion of hydrilla has been a blessing for fish. It provides excellent cover, and concentrates baitfish, aquatic insects and other fish foods. Although hydrilla caused navigation problems, knowledgeable fishermen quickly noted the advantages and took steps to discourage the complete chemical eradication advocated by many lakeshore property owners.

Perhaps some balance can be struck to control vegetation while leaving enough for the fish.

Case Study:
Lake Istokpoga, Florida

In Seminole, the name Istokpoga has a grim meaning — "Man who goes on water dies." Numerous drownings in years past gave the big, windswept lake its reputation. Today, the lake has a reputation for something else — first-rate bass fishing.

Lake Istokpoga (pronounced Is-ta-po´-ga) lies in an old seabed depression. The lake basin and surrounding land are flat, providing no protection when the wind blows.

Although considerably larger than the average Florida natural lake, Istokpoga has many of the qualities of Florida's other prime bass lakes. Its shallow, fertile, tannin-stained waters offer plenty of weedy cover and teem with bass foods such as small sunfish, shad, killifish and golden shiners.

Because Istokpoga averages only 4 feet deep, weeds grow almost everywhere. The shallows have cattails, pickerelweed, bulrushes, maidencane and lily pads.

As in many other Florida lakes, water hyacinth has been a long-standing problem, but has been kept under control with chemicals.

Hydrilla gained a foothold in the early 1980s and spread so rapidly that it crowded out most other kinds of submerged plants. It can take root anywhere, from the shallows to the deepest water, and deep beds may grow nearly to the surface.

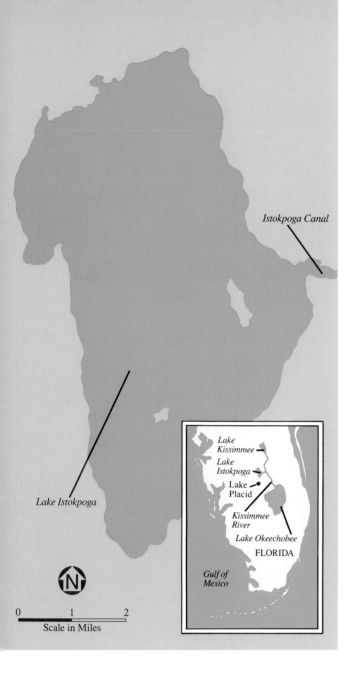

Water hyacinth (top) and hydrilla (bottom) are being controlled by chemicals in Istokpoga

Complaints by boaters and property owners led to an extensive chemical treatment program, but some large hydrilla beds remain. Ongoing chemical control will be necessary to prevent exotic weeds from overrunning the lake.

While hydrilla may be a headache for boaters, it's paradise for largemouth bass. It provides shade and ambush cover for the adults and hiding cover for the young. Within five years after hydrilla got its start in Istokpoga, the bass population tripled.

The lake also supports plenty of good-sized redear sunfish and crappies. Although there are reasonable numbers of bluegills, chain pickerel and channel catfish, these species aren't as popular with anglers.

Istokpoga's water level is regulated by a U.S. Army Corps of Engineers control structure on the canal draining from the southeast corner of the lake. As in

many other Florida lakes, the control structure keeps the water lower than in years past, so the density of vegetation in the shallows has increased. Sediment produced by the decomposing plants is filling in the basin at a much faster rate.

Compared to most Florida lakes, angling pressure on Istokpoga is light. Most anglers fish for bass, with only about half as many pursuing sunfish and crappies.

Lake Istokpoga Physical Data

Acreage	27,692
Average depth	4 ft
Maximum depth	10 ft
Clarity	2 ft
Color	brownish
Total phosphorus (parts per billion)	50
Thermocline	none

Lake Istokpoga Habitat (*sample locations of habitats are numbered on NASA photo*)

1. LILY PADS, called "bonnets," make good spawning habitat for bluegills, redears and crappies. They sometimes draw a few bass.

2. BULRUSH BEDS are spawning areas for bass, sunfish and crappies. You'll find bass in the rushes from October through May.

3. SHELL BEDS hold the small clams and snails (shown) that redear sunfish feed on. The best beds are in 5 to 6½ feet of water, on a slight break.

4. HYDRILLA BEDS hold bass, bluegills, redears and crappies all year. Look for the beds with the lushest, greenest weeds.

5. BOAT CANALS in lakeshore property make good year-round bass and sunfish habitat. Look for the fish around docks and tree roots.

6. CHANNELS cut through stands of emergent vegetation to provide boat access draw largemouths and sunfish at spawning time.

7. CATTAILS (shown), eelgrass and peppergrass attract largemouth bass all year, except during the hottest part of the summer.

8. MAIDENCANE grows only on a sandy bottom and is a good indicator of largemouth spawning habitat. You'll find some bass in it all year.

9. CYPRESS TREES have a complex underwater root network. They hold sunfish all year; bass from April through November.

Lake Istokpoga:
Largemouth Bass

Bass anglers flock to Florida with one thing in mind: catching a trophy bass. Even though bass over 10 pounds are getting harder and harder to find, there's still a reasonable chance of connecting — if you know when, where and how to go about it.

The biggest bass are caught from mid-December through late March, when the fish concentrate near their spawning areas. They spawn on hard, sandy bottoms in stands of emergent vegetation, particularly bulrushes. Most beds are in water from 1½ to 3 feet deep, with at least 4 feet of water nearby.

Spawning activity is light in December but rapidly gains momentum, peaking a few days either side of the first full moon in March. As with all largemouths, the male moves in first and builds the nest; the female hangs back from the nesting area until just before spawning time. Then she swims onto the nest, accompanied by one or more males, and deposits her eggs. Females remain on the nest no more than four days.

Unlike northern largemouths, the female Florida may assist with nest-guarding duties, especially if the male is caught. Many of the largest Florida bass taken are nest-guarding females.

Because the spawning period is so long and not all bass in the lake spawn at the same time, it's possible to catch some bass in the spawning areas and some in typical summertime habitat on the same day.

Golden shiners probably account for more big Floridas than any other bait. They're most effective in winter, but they'll catch bass anytime. Wild shiners work better than those raised in hatcheries. Bass prey on wild shiners in nature, so a hooked shiner gets very nervous when a bass approaches. It skitters to the surface and thrashes about wildly, attracting even uninterested bass. A hatchery shiner, on the other hand, has never seen a bass, so it remains much calmer and triggers fewer strikes.

Shiner fishing can be frustrating. Normally, you'll be fishing in heavy cover, either on the edge of a bulrush or cattail bed, over a mat of hydrilla, or in a weed-fringed canal. A lively shiner will tangle your line around the vegetation, and a hooked bass will swim far back into it, so you'll need heavy tackle. A 7- to 9-foot heavy-power fiberglass rod and a good-sized

LURES for largemouths include: (1) Cordell Boy Howdy, (2) A.C. Shiner 375, (3) Rat-L-Trap, (4) Bomber Model A, (5) tandem spinnerbait, (6) Blue Fox Floyd's Buzzer, (7) 5-inch Ditto Gator Tail, Florida rigged (p. 135).

MAKE a golden shiner rig by sliding on a 3-inch cylinder float and tying on a special weedless shiner hook. Push the hook through the bottom jaw and out the nostril of the shiner (inset). Set the weedguard.

baitcasting reel spooled with 25- to 40-pound abrasion-resistant mono make an ideal combination.

Wild shiners are expensive, but you can catch your own if you know how. To locate shiners, chum shallow weedy areas with oatmeal until you see them dimpling the surface. Then catch them with a cane pole and size 12 hook baited with a tiny doughball, or throw a cast net over them.

Winter fishing usually peaks in midday, when the water temperature is warmest. A slight chop is better than a calm surface; an overcast day better than a sunny one. A warming trend increases feeding activity; a cold front slows feeding and pushes the bass farther back into the rushes or out of the rushes into deeper water.

Fishing for Florida bass on the spawning beds is a highly controversial topic. Many blame this practice for the decline in big bass. When a female bass is on the bed, any disturbance from anglers may cause her to permanently abandon the spawning area. Of course, bass guarding the nest are very aggressive, so many question the sporting ethics of anglers who catch bass when they're most vulnerable.

When the weather warms in summer, wild shiners are tough to keep alive, so almost all anglers use artificials. Most any kind of proven bass lure works — the choice depends on the type of cover, the mood of the bass and personal preference. Serious anglers usually carry several rods rigged with different lures, then experiment to find what the bass want on a given day.

Locating bass in summer can be a challenge in Istokpoga because the lake is so large and has little

structure to concentrate the fish. There are thousands of acres of hydrilla-covered flats, any of which may hold bass.

Your best chances of catching bass are early in the morning, when the temperature is coolest. The fish seem to bite better whenever there's a light to moderate wind.

During an intense heat wave, you'll find largemouths in the thickest hydrilla beds and the deepest bulrushes, where the shade keeps the water a few degrees cooler.

The best summertime approach is to cover a lot of water using a "locator" lure, such as a vibrating plug. Once you catch a fish or two, work the area thoroughly with a lure you can retrieve more slowly, such as a plastic worm or a jig-and-pig. On calm days, topwater lures such as propbaits, buzzbaits and minnow plugs twitched along the surface will draw bass out of the weeds. This artificial lure strategy works just as well other times of the year.

When fishing artificials, use medium- to heavy-power baitcasting or spinning gear with 14- to 17-pound mono. Stout tackle helps extract largemouths from the heavy vegetation. When fishing in hydrilla, for instance, it's not unusual to pull in a bass along with a clump of weeds weighing considerably more than the fish.

Starting in October, you'll see bass busting into schools of shad on the surface. A flock of gulls can be a tipoff; they follow close to pick up the injured shad. It pays to carry an extra rod rigged with a topwater lure or a Rat-L-Trap, should this opportunity present itself.

How to Locate Bass in Hydrilla

CAST a Rat-L-Trap over a hydrilla flat. The weighted lure lets you cast a long way and retrieve rapidly, so you can find active bass quickly.

TOSS a marker when you catch a fish. Continue to work the area with the Rat-L-Trap as long as it continues to produce.

CATCH less aggressive bass, which are often buried deeper in the weeds, by switching to a plastic worm or jig-and-pig.

How to Fish Bass With Golden Shiners

SOUND the outside edges of the bulrush beds with your depth finder, looking for water at least 6 feet deep. Bass prefer the deeper beds.

LOB a shiner rig (p. 133) into pockets in the rushes after anchoring the boat on both ends. If you cast where the rushes are thickest, the shiner will swim around the stems.

PULL your bobber out and try to make it catch on a bulrush stem. This prevents the minnow from pulling the rig far back into the weeds and tangling.

POINT your rod at the fish (left) when you get a bite; reel up slack until you feel weight. Set the hook hard (right) and don't let the fish swim back into the weeds.

Largemouth-Fishing Tips

UNTIE the anchor rope if the bass gets into the weeds. Tie a float to the rope so it doesn't sink. Now you can follow the bass, grab it, then reanchor.

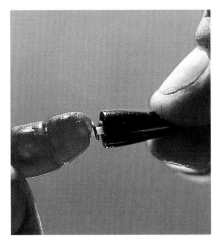

FLORIDA-RIG a worm by twisting a screw-in weight into the head. The weight can't separate, so it pulls the worm deep into the weeds.

TOUGHEN bread for shiner fishing by microwaving a damp, crustless slice for 30 seconds. Roll into a ball and bait a size 12 hook with small bits.

Crappies

When the "specks" are biting on Lake Istokpoga, it's not unusual to catch them a half-dozen at a time. Multiple-line trolling is gaining popularity each year, and for good reason. It enables you to cover a wide swath of water and locate the fish in a hurry. And when you find a school, you'll sometimes catch a fish on every line.

The specks, as they're called by local anglers, are black crappies. They average about a pound, but 2-pounders are not uncommon. There are no white crappies in the lake.

The multi-line technique is simple: Rig up six light spinning outfits (some anglers prefer cane poles) with small jigs or spinnerbaits. Spool up with 10- to 12-pound mono because it's not unusual to hook a big bass. Toss two lines out the back, angle two out the sides from the rear of the boat, then two more out the sides closer to the front. Keep the lines short and troll very slowly in known crappie-producing areas (see opposite page).

You can find crappies throughout the lake, but they tend to concentrate in areas at least 6 feet deep with a light growth of hydrilla on the bottom. Some crappies stay in these areas all year. You'll seldom find them in weed-choked shallows. Even at spawning time, some fish remain in deep water.

Crappies start to spawn in late January. They clear spawning beds in the bulrushes or lily pads and you can catch them by dabbling small jigs or minnows into pockets in the weeds. Spawning peaks during the full moon in February and continues until mid-March.

The fish bite best from November through April, with the peak from December through February. Fishing slows considerably during the summer.

Many of the best catches come at night. Simply anchor in a deep hole at dusk, toss out a small minnow beneath a bobber, and wait for the fish to start biting. The action usually starts about an hour after dark. Fishing is best on the darkest nights, either around the new moon or when the moon is covered by clouds.

Some Istokpoga night-fishing enthusiasts have developed a sure-fire crappie system. They use a pontoon boat rigged with a generator to provide power for strong lights that shine into the water, attracting insects which fall to the surface and draw minnows. The crappies soon follow. Some feel that the vibration of the generator also attracts crappies.

How to Night-Fish for Crappies

ANCHOR over a deep hole, then set extension poles with bobber rigs in each of the rod holders. The rigs (inset) have an orange float for visibility, split-shot and a 1½- to 2-inch minnow on a size 1 Aberdeen hook. Set the float so the minnow is about 3 feet off bottom, then tighten the line so the float moves when the boat swings on the anchor. When a crappie bites, the pole gives enough that the fish won't feel resistance and spit the hook.

How to Troll With Multiple Lines

LURES include: (1) Mister Twister Teeny jig, (2) Napier Sand Hornet, (3) Napier Sand Hornet with spinner, (4) Bass Buster Super Beetle Twist.

TROLL slowly through a likely crappie area with several rods secured in rod holders. Set the front rods widest, the middle rods next widest, and the rear rods narrowest. Keep all lines at the same length, 25 to 30 feet behind the boat. This way, the lines won't tangle, even if you turn sharply.

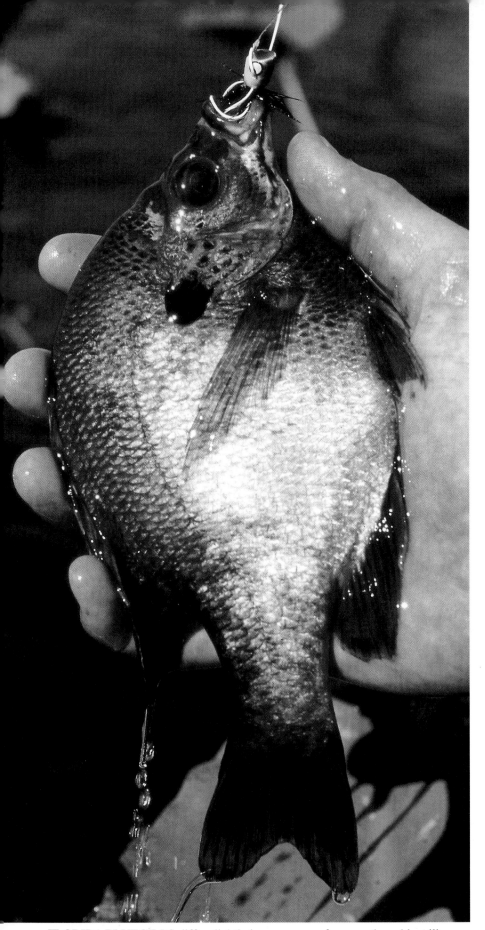

FLORIDA BLUEGILLS differ slightly in appearance from northern bluegills. The entire body has a bluish cast, sometimes with dark vertical bars, and the adult male (shown) has a small, copper-colored patch on the forehead.

Lake Istokpoga:
Sunfish

You can catch sunfish almost anywhere in the shallows of Lake Istokpoga. Redears, or "shellcrackers," predominate, but there's a good population of bluegills as well.

The largest concentrations of shellcrackers — and the biggest fish — are found on the shell beds. As their name suggests, shellcrackers feed heavily on small clams and snails. The pharyngeal teeth in the throat act as a grinder, crushing the shells. The beds attract shellcrackers year around, except during the spawning period.

Veteran Lake Istokpoga anglers locate the shell beds by probing the bottom with a cane pole. Usually, the beds are in 5 to 6½ feet of water. You'll know you're in the right area when the bottom is firm and you can feel the shells crunch. Normally, the best shell beds are on a slight break with little or no weed growth.

All the shell beds hold fish, but only certain ones draw good-sized shellcrackers. If you're catching a lot of small fish, you probably won't catch many big ones, so keep moving until you find fish running ¾ to 1¼ pounds. Istokpoga's shellcrackers grow as large as 2 pounds.

Once you find a likely spot, anchor your boat within easy casting distance. Rig up a bullet-sinker rig (opposite page), cast out a couple of red wigglers, and wait for a bite. If the fish are around, you won't wait long.

REDEAR SUNFISH, or shellcrackers, are pale green and have a red margin along the entire rear edge of the "ear."

The pumpkinseed, by contrast, has a small red spot on the tip of the ear and bluish streaks on the cheek.

Slip-sinker fishing works better than bobber fishing because shellcrackers look for their food right on the bottom. If you prefer to bobber-fish, set your float so the bait rides no more than a few inches up.

The shell beds normally have few snags, so you can get by with light tackle. Most anglers use light spinning outfits with 4- to 6-pound mono. Long-shank hooks are a must; shellcrackers often swallow the bait so deep that you can't even see the hook.

Shellcrackers spawn in lily pads or bulrushes, or on a sandy bottom just outside of them. Spawning starts in April, peaks in May and June and continues until September. The males excavate small beds around plant roots, usually at a depth of 2 to 3 feet. You'll often find a large colony of beds in a small area, but they may be hard to see in the brownish water.

Fishing shellcrackers on the spawning beds is really not much different than fishing them on the shell beds. Use a bullet-sinker rig baited with wigglers and cast into the bedding area.

When they're bedding, shellcrackers bite best around the full moon; when they're not, the action is better around the dark of the moon.

LURES AND RIGS include: (1) slip-sinker rig with a ⅛-ounce bullet sinker, a split-shot for a stop and a size 4 Aberdeen hook baited with two red wigglers; (2) Gaines Minnie-Pop popper; (3) Blue-winged Olive wet fly.

Wade-fishing for spawning shellcrackers is popular in warm weather. Anchor your boat near a known spawning area and jump in. Stay far enough from the beds that you don't spook the fish. This technique allows you to approach the fish more quietly and keeps you cool.

Shellcrackers bite any time of year, but most are caught from May through August. You'll catch more fish in midday than early or late in the day.

Most anglers prefer warm, clear weather with enough wind to create a light chop.

Bluegills in Istokpoga run just as big as the shell-crackers. They're easiest to catch in May and June, the peak spawning months, especially around the full moon.

Like shellcrackers, bluegills often spawn in large colonies. Although you'll find bluegill and shellcracker colonies in the same vicinity, you won't find bluegill beds in shellcracker colonies or vice versa.

You'll catch bluegills using shellcracker tactics, but 'gills prefer crickets and grass shrimp to worms. Fly-fishing with wet flies and poppers also works well.

Tips for Finding and Catching Sunfish

LOOK for spawning beds while drifting or slow-trolling through shallow weedy areas (left). Be sure to wear polarized sunglasses. Most of the beds are in less than 3 feet of water. When you find some beds, keep your boat at a distance and use a cane pole to lower your bait to the fish (right).

POKE the bottom with a long pole to find shell beds. You should be able to feel the shells cracking once you locate a bed.

TRY grass shrimp to catch bluegills and shellcrackers. You can find the small crustaceans by picking through clumps of water hyacinth.

USE an extra-long-shank hook so you can unhook sunfish more easily. Even if the fish is hooked deep, you can still grab the end of the hook to push it free.

Lake Istokpoga:
Other Species

Few Lake Istokpoga anglers fish for anything other than bass, sunfish and crappies, but the lake also holds good populations of chain pickerel and channel catfish. And you may encounter a curious fish seldom seen by freshwater anglers, the needlefish. These slender, toothy fish originally swam in from the sea and now reproduce in the lake. Crappie anglers commonly take them while fishing with small minnows.

When fishing for largemouth, you'll often catch chain pickerel. They hang out in the same locations and strike the same lures. They're excellent eating if you remove the bothersome Y-bones.

Shellcracker anglers sometimes hook channel cats when bottom-fishing with worms. Most cats, however, are taken on trotlines.

NEEDLEFISH have a skinny bill about one-fourth the length of the body; it's filled with tiny, but very sharp, teeth. Most needlefish measure 12 to 16 inches in length, but a few reach 22 inches.

CHANNEL CATFISH average about 5 pounds in Istokpoga, but some reach 25. They have a deeply forked tail, and the smaller ones commonly have scattered black spots.

CHAIN PICKEREL are easy to identify because of the chain-link markings on the side. Lake Istokpoga pickerel run 2 to 3 pounds, with a few up to 5 pounds.

Oxbow Lakes

These river-channel lakes offer first-rate fishing, but anglers must contend with constantly changing water levels

If you live near a big, winding river, you're probably not too far from Horseshoe, Crescent or Half-Moon Lake. Dozens of lakes with these names are found throughout the country, remnants of riverbeds left behind when the river changed course.

The term "oxbow" originates from the name of the U-shaped device used to collar oxen to their yoke. Oxbow lakes have the same shape because of the way they were formed.

A river flowing over loose materials continually erodes the outside bends and deposits silt on the inside bends, causing the channel to wind, or meander. The river forms a series of loops, some of which erode completely through at the neck (p. 10). The crescent-shaped body of water that remains is usually isolated from the river, though some remain connected on the downstream end.

Most oxbow lakes form naturally, but sometimes man speeds up the process for purposes of navigation or flood control. Meander loops are often cut off to shorten the channel or to allow flood waters to pass more quickly, reducing upstream flooding.

Oxbow lakes have a very short life span, sometimes less than 50 years. A few persist for as long as 1,000 years, still a short life compared to other types of natural lakes. When the river tops its banks, it deposits silt in the upper end of the lake. The lake gradually fills in until it becomes too shallow for fish. Eventually, it becomes nothing more than a swampy scar on the landscape.

Rivers constantly change and new oxbows form as fast as old ones fill in. But on many of the country's largest rivers, the banks have been stabilized and the channel has been straightened for commercial navigation. The rivers cannot meander, so no new oxbows form as old oxbows die.

Because of their short life span and their tendency to flood, oxbows are not as heavily developed as other natural lakes. Government agencies and private investors are reluctant to spend money on a lake where the future is so uncertain. Most oxbow lakes have few, if any, resorts or private cabins, and some lack public accesses.

You may be able to motor into the lake from the river, if there is a connection at the lower end. If not, consult a U. S. Geological Survey quad map or Corps of Engineers river chart to determine where the lake comes closest to the present river channel. Then, you can portage a canoe or small boat from the river to the lake.

Oxbow lakes rise and fall with the river. Even without a connecting channel, the lake level follows the river level because of seepage through the highly

porous soil. If the seepage rate is slow, however, the change in lake level may lag considerably behind that of the river.

In oxbow lakes that connect to the river, fish swim freely between the two so they usually have the same kinds of fish. In oxbows that do not have a connecting channel, fish from the river swim into the lake during floods.

Oxbow lakes will challenge anglers who aren't accustomed to constantly changing water levels. When the water is high, the fish scatter into newly flooded lowlands. When it's low, they're often confined in small, deep basins of the lake. Veteran oxbow lake anglers know where to look for fish at different times of year at different water stages.

But oxbows offer some advantages over other types of lakes. Because of their crescent shape, you can always find a spot out of the wind. Another bonus: the lack of access and resort facilities means relatively light angling pressure, so oxbow lakes still in their prime offer outstanding fishing. Even if the lake is heavily fished, it is restocked every time the river overflows its banks.

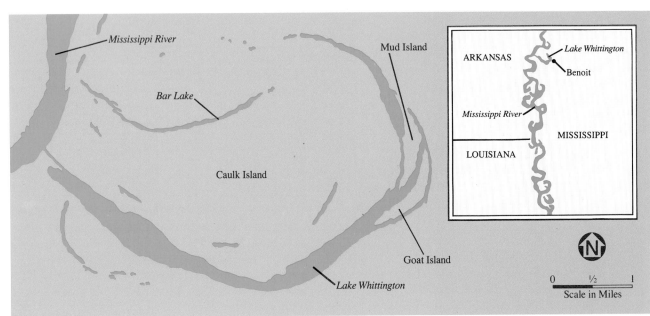

Mississippi River

Mud Island

Bar Lake

Caulk Island

Goat Island

Lake Whittington

ARKANSAS

Lake Whittington

Benoit

Mississippi River

MISSISSIPPI

LOUISIANA

N

0   ½   1
Scale in Miles

In 1937, the Corps of Engineers bulldozed a channel (arrow) to cut off Lake Whittington from the Mississippi River

Case Study:

Lake Whittington, Mississippi

Oxbow lakes abound in the lower Mississippi River valley, particularly from southern Missouri south to the delta. Here, the flood plain is very flat and sandy, so the river can easily erode its banks and change course. Because the river has such a large flow in its lower reaches, its cutting ability is great.

Between Cape Girardeau, Missouri, and New Orleans, are 37 major oxbow lakes. Typical of these is Lake Whittington, a 2,350-acre oxbow near Benoit, Mississippi. Like many of these waters, Whittington is a "cutoff" lake. It was isolated from the river when the Corps of Engineers cut through the neck of a 15-mile meander loop to create a shortcut for barge traffic. Erosion would have cut off the loop in another decade or two; the Corps simply sped up the process.

Lake Whittington is bounded on the south and east by the Mississippi River levee, and on the north and west by Caulk Island, the piece of land left behind after the cutoff. As in most oxbows, the upper end of the lake has silted in and is completely separated from the river unless the water gets extremely high. The lower end is open, and the channel to the river is navigable unless the water is very low.

In an average year, the water level in Lake Whittington fluctuates about 30 feet. The water level usually peaks in April, rising about 25 feet above normal summer levels. It may rise 45 feet in a severe flood. The level is usually lowest in September and October, when it drops about 5 feet below normal. Levels 10 feet below normal have been recorded.

During floods, water covers much of Caulk Island, and fish spread out over thousands of acres of partially submerged trees and brush. Fishing can be good during high water, but navigating through the timber requires a maneuverable, shallow-draft boat. Most local anglers prefer 14- to 16-foot jon boats powered by 15- to 25-hp outboards. A push pole is a must for crossing shallow spots and breaking through logjams.

Because the clarity is so low and the water level changes so often, aquatic vegetation does not have a chance to take root. Fish rely on logs, brush and rip-rap for cover.

In summer, water more than 20 feet deep lacks sufficient oxygen for gamefish. Most of the lake is so shallow that wind circulation keeps the temperature the same from top to bottom.

The lake supports good populations of crappies, bluegills, largemouth bass, white bass and channel catfish. There's also a fair number of longear and redear sunfish, some yellow bass, and a few sea-run striped bass. Although silt deposits have reduced the water volume by 60 percent since the lake was created, fishing has held up well.

Local fishermen are concerned about Lake Whittington's future because the lake has filled in so rapidly in recent years. Many believe that a dam is needed at the lower end to keep water levels higher during low-water periods. At present, however, neither state nor federal conservation agencies have any such plans.

Lake Whittington Physical Data	
Acreage	2,350
Average depth	8 ft
Maximum depth	56 ft
Clarity	1 ft
Color	brown
Total phosphorus (parts per billion)	120
Thermocline	none
Average date of freeze-up	rarely freezes

Lake Whittington Habitat (*sample locations of habitats are numbered on NASA photo*)

1. THE OUTLET CHANNEL holds large schools of white bass, as well as some largemouths and catfish, from summer through fall.

2. CLEARINGS along shore indicate a clean bottom where crappies, bass and bluegills spawn. With no trees, the sun can easily warm the beds.

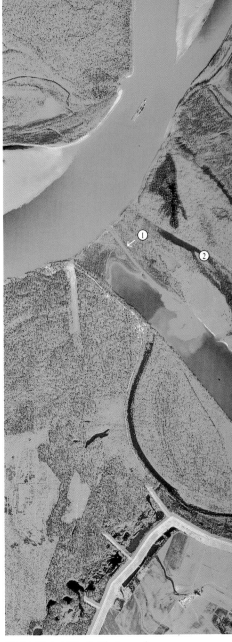

NASA High Altitude Photograph

3. YOUNG WILLOWS sprout up when silted-in flats are exposed at low water. When the water rises, the flooded shoots make good gamefish cover.

4. RIPRAP banks along the main lake, especially those with submerged trees or brush for cover, draw largemouths from summer through fall.

5. FLOATING DEBRIS loosened by rising water provides cover for bass and crappies. The wind determines where the debris will settle.

6. BUCKBRUSH clumps provide cover for all fish species in high water. Fish can easily hide among the tangle of branches and leaves.

7. POINTS in the main lake attract largemouths, crappies and sunfish in summer; the shallow flats atop the points hold white bass.

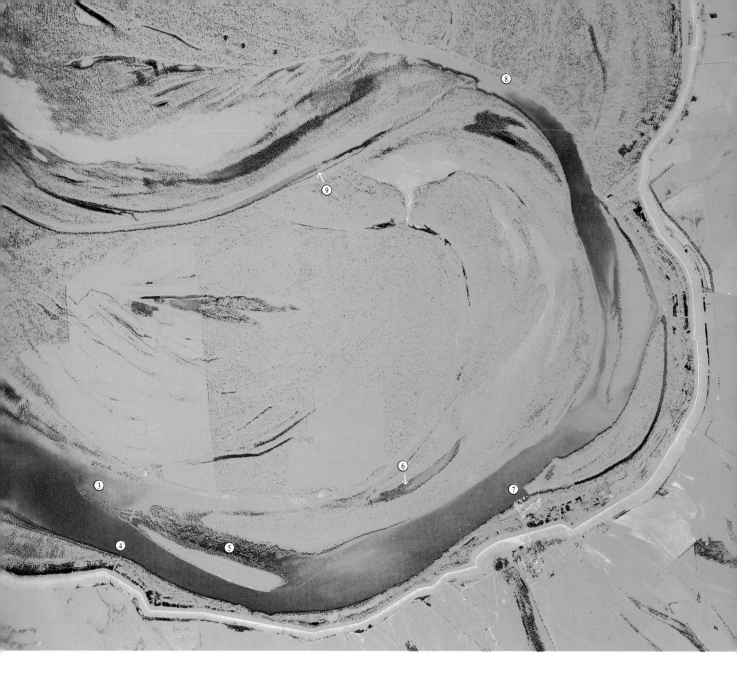

8. MATURE WILLOWS offer cover to largemouth bass, bluegills and crappies during high water. Most of the fish hold in the outer few rows of trees, rather than in the middle of the flooded stand.

9. EARTHEN DAMS are built to maintain water levels in backwaters during low-water periods. When flooded, the dams provide structure which attracts bluegills and largemouth bass.

Lake Whittington:

Crappies

It's a good idea to test your drag before going after crappies in Lake Whittington. Crappies aren't known as powerful fighters, but when you hook one pushing 2 pounds, it'll give you all the tussle you can handle with light gear.

Like most other oxbows in the lower Mississippi valley, Lake Whittington supports both black and white crappies, with whites predominating. It's not unusual for anglers to catch hefty stringers of 1- to 2-pounders, and occasionally someone lands one over 3.

Crappies bite best in spring, around spawning time. The action starts in early March, peaks in early April, then tapers off by mid-May. Normally, the lake is high this time of year, so most of the crappies move into the backwaters. Some congregate along the banks of the main lake.

Before spawning, crappies stage along the outside edges of flooded timber and brush along the shoreline. As spawning time approaches, they move closer to shore. Often, they'll spawn in open areas among the trees and brush, usually at depths of 6 feet or less.

"Tightlining" (opposite page) with $\frac{1}{16}$- to $\frac{1}{48}$-ounce jigs is the best way to catch crappies around spawning time. You can also catch them by tightlining a split-shot and minnow or fishing a minnow beneath a bobber.

A 10- to 12-foot extension pole rigged with 4- to 6-pound mono is ideal for tightlining. The long pole enables you to reach into tight spots where you can't

How to Tightline for Crappies

1. TIE on a $\frac{1}{16}$- to $\frac{1}{48}$-ounce jig and slide the knot to the top of the eye so the jig hangs horizontally. Adjust the knot often; if it slips to the front of the eye (inset), the jig rides vertically and looks unnatural.

2. SCULL with a short paddle to slowly move the boat through likely crappie water. You can best control the boat by sculling from the front end. Sculling allows precise boat control and is even quieter than an electric motor.

3. HOLD your rod steady as the boat moves along. Crappies prefer a steady swimming motion to an erratic jigging action. Usually, the fish are within a foot of the bottom, but you'll have to experiment to find the right depth.

4. COMPARE depth settings when one angler starts catching crappies. Other anglers in the boat should adjust their lines to fish at exactly the same depth. Sometimes a few inches can make a big difference.

cast. Make sure the pole has a small reel with a drag; otherwise a big crappie could snap your line.

Good springtime fishing requires warm, stable weather. When conditions are right, the fish will bite throughout the day. A cold front or rapidly changing water levels will push crappies out of their spawning areas.

As the water level subsides, crappies in the backwaters move back to the main lake. You'll find most of the fish around woody cover on points, along steep banks, and on old river channel drop-offs. The most productive summertime depths are 6 to 12 feet. Manmade brush piles, or "crappie mats," also attract fish, and some crappies suspend over deep water, usually at depths of 12 feet or less.

Tightlining works just as well in summer, but you'll have to fish deeper than in spring. Keep your line as close to vertical as possible, and experiment to find the right depth.

Fishing in midsummer can be tough because crappies are widely scattered and natural food such as shad and plankton is plentiful. To locate the fish, some anglers troll up to 10 rods rigged with jigs of different colors and sizes. The jigs run at different depths, and when a pattern emerges, they switch all rods to match whatever is working. Summertime fishing is best on overcast days.

Crappie fishing picks up when the water starts to cool in mid-October. Where you find the fish depends mainly on the weather and the water level. If the water is high and the weather mild, they'll move into shallow trees and brush to feed and you can fish for them the same way you would in the spring. If the water is low and the weather cold, they'll go as deep as 30 feet, but you can still catch them by trolling with jigs. The technique is identical to that used in midsummer, but you'll need heavier jigs, up to $\frac{1}{8}$-ounce. Trolling in deep water continues to produce crappies through the winter.

Lake Whittington:

Bluegills

Most Mississippi River oxbows hold plenty of bluegills, and Lake Whittington is no exception. When the fish are concentrated in their spawning areas, you can easily catch several dozen ½- to 1-pounders in a day.

Bluegills spawn later in the season than crappies. Spawning starts in late April, peaks from mid-May to mid-June and continues into early August.

May and June are the best fishing months because males are

RIGS include: (1) bobber rig and size 8 extra-long-shank hook with cricket threaded on, (2) slip-bobber rig with a size 8 hook and red wiggler.

aggressively guarding their nests, attacking any intruders — including an angler's bait.

Springtime high water draws spawners into the same backwaters that attract crappies. You may catch bluegills when fishing for crappies, but the majority of the bluegills are in shallower water.

The key to catching springtime bluegills is locating a large spawning bed containing a cluster of nests. Look for beds in water from 1 to 4 feet deep, around the roots of a tree or in an opening in brushy cover.

When you find a productive spawning bed, be sure to note its location carefully because bluegills will return year after year, assuming the water level is about the same.

The basic bluegill rig consists of a 12- to 16-foot cane or extension pole; 4- to 10-pound mono, depending on the type of cover; a small float; split-shot; and an extra-long-shank size 6 or 8 hook. The long pole works well for placing your bait into small pockets in the brush. The long hook is ideal for stringing on crickets or cockroaches, the preferred baits. It also keeps

bluegills from swallowing the hook, so you can unhook them more quickly.

If there are a lot of overhanging branches, a light spinning outfit works better than an extension pole. Keeping your rod tip low to the water, you can toss a slip-bobber rig beneath the obstruction (see below). Some anglers carry an extension pole and a spinning rod so they can fish any type of cover.

The techniques used in spring will produce bluegills all year, although the locations may differ. When the water level drops, the fish move back to the main lake. You'll find them around logs, floating debris and riprap, usually near deep water. They remain in these areas all winter, assuming the water stays low. If it rises, they'll return to their springtime locations.

Bluegills bite best in warm, stable weather when the water level is holding steady or falling slowly. A fast rise or fall will scatter the fish, and a fast rise will muddy the water as well.

You can catch bluegills any time of day, but in summer, mornings and evenings are usually best.

How to Find Bluegills During the Spawning Season

LOOK for spawning beds at the base of locust trees. Also called "thorn trees" because of the long thorns on the branches and trunk, the trees shade out other plants, giving bluegills an open area to spawn.

CRUISE the shoreline, casting to openings in brushy cover, tree roots or other likely spawning areas. If the fish are there, they'll bite in seconds. It's not unusual to catch 20 or 30 from a single bed.

How to Fish Tight Spots

LOWER a bobber rig into a small pocket in the brush using a 12- to 16-foot extension pole or cane pole. When you hook a fish, the long pole enables you to lift it out vertically, so it doesn't tangle in the brush.

FLIP a bobber rig beneath overhanging limbs to reach an open pocket. A short spinning rod with a light tip is ideal for this type of casting; keep the rod tip low and cast with a sharp backhand or sidearm motion.

Largemouth Bass

Because of the rapidly changing water levels, largemouths in oxbow lakes have developed an unusual feeding pattern seldom seen by anglers on other types of lakes.

In spring, rising water floods thousands of acres of timber and brush, forcing terrestrial animals such as snakes and mice to swim for cover. Bass roam freely through the woody tangle, picking these animals off the surface.

Faced with the maze of cover, anglers tend to select snag-resistant lures such as plastic worms, brushguard jigs or spinnerbaits. But these offerings seldom work as well as surface lures, which better imitate the natural food.

Fishing really heats up in late April and stays hot through June. Most of the fish run 1 to 3 pounds, but there are plenty of 4- to 6-pounders and every so often, somebody lands one weighing more than 8 pounds.

Any propbait, stickbait or minnow plug will work, but one of the local favorites is a minnow plug with a propeller on the tail. You can buy the lures (Bagley's Spinner Tail) or make your own (p. 154). Using a medium-power spinning or baitcasting outfit with 8- to 12-pound mono, toss the lure past a tree or clump of brush and retrieve with twitches sharp enough to make the prop churn the surface. Pause occasionally and let the lure rest a few seconds, particularly when it reaches a pocket in the cover.

You'll improve your odds by selecting the right type of cover. Bare trees seldom hold bass, but those with a lot of vines or small branches around the trunk provide good ambush spots. Trees and brush near the edge of a flooded stand usually hold more bass than those deep within the stand.

You can score consistently with this surface-fishing technique, if the water is at the right stage. Lake Whittington anglers frequently check the closest water level gauge on the river. Fishing is best when it registers between 16 and 25 feet and is holding steady or slowly rising or falling. If it rises too rapidly, the water gets muddy; if it falls too quickly, the fish don't feed.

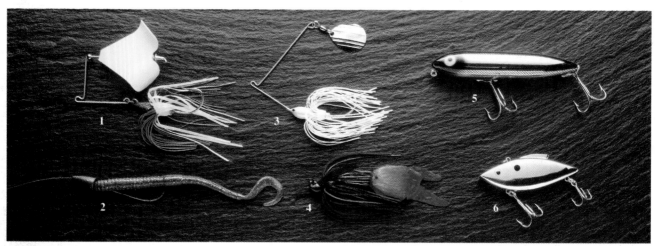

LURES for Lake Whittington largemouth bass include: (1) Bass Pro Shop Rocker Buzz buzzbait, (2) 6-inch T's Salt Hookers worm rigged Texas style with a 2/0 hook, (3) Strike King spinnerbait, (4) 5/16-ounce Stanley Jig with pork frog, (5) Heddon Zara Spook, (6) Bill Lewis Rat-L-Trap.

By early summer, the water has usually dropped enough to force bass out of the timber and brush and into the main lake. When the river gauge reads 10 to 15 feet, you'll find most fish near points, steep banks, riprapped shorelines, breaks along the old river channel or shoreline springs. The best spots have some type of woody cover and are usually less than 10 feet deep, with deeper water nearby. Bass will stay in these locations as long as the water is stable or slowly falling.

In summer and fall, use standard largemouth-fishing tactics. When searching for bass, cast a spinnerbait or buzzbait. In dense woody cover, try a plastic worm or jig-and-pig. On points or other open-water structure with lighter cover, toss a crankbait. Most anglers use medium- to heavy-power baitcasting tackle with 12- to 20-pound mono, depending on the type of cover they're fishing. By the middle of December, the rapidly cooling water pushes largemouths deeper and fishing slows until the weather begins to warm again in mid-March.

Warm, stable weather and overcast skies spell fast bass action on Lake Whittington. Throughout most of the year, the fish bite best early and late in the day, but springtime fishing is better from midday to late afternoon.

How to Fish a Doctored Minnow Plug

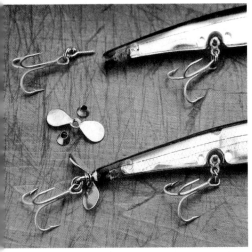

REMOVE the rear screw from a minnow plug. Slip a propbait propeller and a pair of cup washers over the screw and reattach it.

CAST well past the cover where you suspect bass are holding. Angle your cast so the lure will track as close to the cover as possible.

TWITCH the plug sharply as you retrieve, letting it rest a few seconds between twitches. The erratic action will draw bass from several feet down.

CAST into patches of duckweed. The small floating plants attract bass if they're packed together tightly enough to provide heavy shade.

LOOK for viney trees or trees with lots of branches on the trunk. They're more likely to hold bass than are trees with a bare trunk.

154

Lake Whittington:

White Bass

If you like fast action, try white bass fishing in a Mississippi River oxbow. When conditions are right, you can easily catch 100 fish a day.

From June through August, when water from Lake Whittington is draining into the Mississippi, big schools of white bass move into the outlet channel to feed on the young shad that congregate there.

When bass are in the channel, look for them in small eddies created by points and indentations along the shoreline, and in the large eddy that forms where the channel meets the Mississippi River. They also school up on sandbars and points in the main lake.

White bass are easy to find; all you have to do is look for the surface commotion created when they bust into the shad schools. Then, using light spinning gear with 6-pound mono, simply cast a crankbait, jig or tailspin into the melee. The bass average over a pound, and some weigh 2 pounds.

LURES include: (1) Rebel Fastrac Minnow, (2) Rattl'n Rap, (3) Mann's Little George, (4) Baby Torpedo, (5) ¼-ounce Mister Twister Sassy Shad.

Index